THE LOSS OF
THE TITANIC

THE LOSS OF THE TITANIC

'I Survived the TITANIC'

LAWRENCE BEESLEY

AMBERLEY

Originally published in 1912 as *The Loss of the RMS Titanic: Its Story and Its Lessons*

This illustrated edition first published 2011

Amberley Publishing
The Hill, Stroud,
Gloucestershire, GL5 4EP

www.amberleybooks.com

Copyright © The Estate of Lawrence Beesley, 1912, 1979, 2011

The right of Lawrence Beesley to be identified as the Author of this work has been asserted in accordance with the Copyrights, Designs and Patents Act 1988.

ISBN 978 1 4456 0443 5

British Library Cataloguing in Publication Data. A catalogue record for this book is available from the British Library.

Typeset in 10pt on 12pt Sabon.
Typesetting and Origination by Amberley Publishing.
Printed in the UK.

Contents

Preface to Centenary Edition

On 10 April 1912, my grandfather Lawrence Beesley boarded a ship in Southampton, bound for New York. He had paid £13 for a second class ticket, and planned to visit his youngest brother Arthur, then living in Toronto.

Five days later, he became one of the few men to escape from a historic disaster, the sinking of the *Titanic* after it brushed against an iceberg while running at full speed. Arriving in New York he wrote, in six weeks, an account that vividly described the drama of his escape, the terrible fate of those unable to find space on a lifeboat, and the technical and managerial flaws that contributed to the accident.

His book, *The Loss of the RMS Titanic,* is a classic account of disaster at sea. It has been constantly in print because of the intense interest the tragedy aroused. A luxury liner, built with advanced technology and carrying wealthy and famous passengers, had met with unparalleled disaster on its maiden voyage. Of its 2,223 passengers and crew, 1,517 perished. But the tragedy was no act of God. It was through human folly that the

Titanic carried too few lifeboats, that she was not properly equipped to spot icebergs at night, and that her captain drove her at full speed while ignoring several warnings of an ice field in her path. The catastrophe was a monument to the destruction that can be brought about by technology and miscalculation, presaging the even greater disaster from the same cause that was to break out two years later in the First World War.

My grandfather was an ordinary individual caught in the throes of a historic event. But he was not a passive agent in his survival. Had he not been keenly aware of his surroundings, and kept his head during a few crucial minutes, he would have perished as did 92 per cent of the male passengers travelling in second class.

Lawrence Beesley was born on 31 December 1877, in Wirksworth, Derbyshire. It was in this ancient town that Richard Arkwright, the inventor of the water frame and other cotton-processing machines, and a pioneer of the Industrial Revolution, built one of his first factories. Lawrence's father, Henry Beesley, was a disciplinarian who often beat his children, and they in turn showed him respect rather than affection. Henry was the manager of the Arkwright bank in Wirksworth. That was not his only association with the Arkwright family. After Henry's death in 1907, Lawrence learned that his father was the illegitimate son of Albert Arkwright, Richard Arkwright's great-grandson who lived at the Gate House in Wirksworth. Henry's mother, Anne Wigley, was the daughter of a gardener on the Arkwright estate.

Lawrence was educated at Cambridge University where he studied science and discovered a species of algae, named *Ulvella beesleyi*. While still an undergraduate he married Gertrude Cecile Macbeth with whom he had a son, Alec. (Alec grew up to be an accountant, then married Dodie Smith, a playwright and author of *I Capture the Castle* and *The Hundred and One Dalmations*.)

My grandfather graduated with first class honours in natural science and decided to become a science teacher. His first job was teaching back home at Wirksworth, and he then moved to Dulwich College in London. Around this time he developed a keen interest in Christian Science. This was a perhaps surprising departure for a science teacher, given that Christian Scientists assign priority to spiritual healing over scientifically based medicine. In 1909 he resigned from Dulwich College and set up practice in London as a Christian Science healer.

During the *Titanic*'s voyage, my grandfather took a keen interest in every detail of the ship, noticing for instance that it listed slightly to port, and that vibration increased as the ship picked up speed during the night of 14 April. The deadly brush with the iceberg was imperceptible to the passengers, but Lawrence was at once alert when the propellers stopped and he climbed from his cabin to the top deck to see what had happened.

His escape, according to his account, evidently lay in his thinking differently from the crowd. The *Titanic* hit the iceberg at 11.40 p.m. on 14 April, and sank at 2.20 a.m. the following morning. The enormous ship was turning at the moment of impact and avoided a head-on collision, only to have an underwater extension of the iceberg incise a 300-foot gash in its metal walls. The *Titanic* was designed to stay afloat with four of its forward sections flooded, but could not sustain the compromise of six.

Shortly after midnight, barely twenty minutes later, Captain Smith ordered the lifeboats to be readied, presumably because he realised that the ship would founder. This knowledge was not shared with the passengers. Probably to prevent panic, they were left in ignorance that the ship was doomed and that there were not enough lifeboats.

The first public hint of this impending tragedy came when the crew ordered men and women to be separated, a strong pointer that women and children would be given priority in leaving the ship. A rumour went around the starboard side of the ship that all men were to be taken off on the port side, and almost all the men on deck crossed over to port. Only Lawrence and two others remained on the starboard side of the ship. Then, as he watched a lifeboat full of women being lowered to the sea, a crew member called up from the boat, asking Lawrence if there were any women left on his deck. When he said no, the crew member said, 'Then you had better jump.' My grandfather was thus able to step clear of the stricken ship.

So what made Lawrence stay starboard, a decision which led to his survival, when almost all the other men went portside to their perdition? The explanation he gives in his book is not entirely satisfying. 'I can personally think of no decision arising from reasoned thought that induced me to remain rather than to cross over,' he writes. Perhaps anticipating the reader's thought that some conscious decision would be required to avoid following the crowd, he adds a further sentence, which also falls short of providing an illuminating explanation: 'But while there was no process of conscious reason at work, I am convinced that what was my salvation was a recognition of the necessity of being quiet and waiting in patience for some opportunity of safety to present itself.'

While many passengers were at first reluctant to leave the ship, Lawrence had noticed early on that something was seriously amiss. As he ran down a flight of stairs shortly after the collision, he writes, he felt 'a curious sense of something out of balance and of not being able to put one's feet down in the right place.' Later, when the crew took the drastic step of separating wives from their husbands, Lawrence perhaps grasped the implication that there were not enough lifeboats. If so, he may have concluded that being among a throng of men offered the lowest chance of survival and he would therefore be better off away from the crowd. But he would perhaps have been unwilling to describe such a cold calculation in print, even though it would not have been unethical; his place in the lifeboat was not obtained at anyone else's expense.

An extraordinary postscript to Lawrence's narrative relates to the receipt he received after checking his valuables with the *Titanic*'s purser. The receipt, which looks like one half of a baggage label, was before him as he wrote his book. It bore the words 'White Star Line, RMS *Titanic*' and the number 208. The other half of the label was attached to the envelope holding his money. 'Along with other similar envelopes it may still be intact in the safe at the bottom of the sea,' Lawrence wrote.

One day in May 1995 I received a call from a historian, Michael A. Findlay, who was examining the artefacts recently salvaged from the *Titanic*'s wreck site. One of them was a label with the words 'White Star Line, RMS *Titanic*, 208.' Mr Findlay had recognised it as the match to my grandfather's receipt. Along with other documents it had been removed from the purser's safe and stuffed into a Gladstone bag.

I don't know what became of the receipt that remained in Lawrence's possession. Its counterpart, buried for more than eighty years in 12,500 feet of water 400 miles off the coast of Newfoundland, was evidently in the safer place.

On his return from the United States Lawrence resumed his career as a Christian Science practitioner. He joined the Psychical Research Society. His first wife, Gertrude, had died in 1906 and in 1919 he married his second wife, Muriel Greenwood, formerly Brownjohn. Muriel had three daughters before her marriage to Lawrence – Vera, Dinah and my mother Laurien. But Laurien always said that Lawrence was her biological father, and I see no reason to doubt her.

Besides the similarities of their looks and first names is the fact that Lawrence assigned Laurien the same birthday as his – 31 December – which she believed was not the true date, although probably close to it. After his marriage to Muriel, Lawrence had two more children with her, Waveney and Hugh.

Lawrence was not an ideal father. He was estranged from his son Alec, who felt his father neglected him. My mother, whose spelling was always idiosyncratic, often complained that Lawrence failed to provide a proper education, taking his children to the golf course when they should have been in school.

He made them participate in another of his hobbies, the chasing of fires. At the first sound of the fire alarm he would pile all the children into his car and take off after the fire engine. The firemen were not really happy with his attentions. But they could not dismiss him as a mere nuisance after an occasion when they arrived at the scene of the fire to find their hose was missing. This vital piece of equipment had dropped off the fire engine during its journey. A few minutes later Lawrence and family drove up along with the hose that they had retrieved along the way.

Lawrence eventually gave up his Christian Science practice and reverted to education. In 1934 he bought and ran a school in Bexhill for boys aged five to fourteen. It was at this school that my father Michael arrived as a tutor and where he met my mother Laurien. Both were interested in the stage. Laurien had begun a promising acting career and Michael had written several plays, one of which was to have been performed in London but production was cancelled on the outbreak of the Second World War.

Michael's relationship with his father-in-law was not one of unalloyed respect. He used to tell the story of how Lawrence, as headmaster of the school, decided one day to embark on a series of Sunday sermons about the Ten Commandments. Michael wondered if Lawrence had realised he would soon need to explain what adultery was to his innocent young charges. He need not have worried. When the seventh Sunday came around, Lawrence blandly announced that he was about to talk of a grave sin, that of adulteration, as in watering down the milk. Reflecting on Lawrence's personal situation with respect to the Commandment's actual words, Michael had serious difficulty during the sermon in maintaining the composure expected of a junior master.

Lawrence was often consulted by historians arguing over the events of the *Titanic*'s sinking and by film-makers re-enacting them. On one occasion he and Laurien were invited to the film set of *A Night to Remember*, a 1958 docudrama based on a book of the same title by Walter Lord. For some reason Lawrence decided that it was not enough merely to observe the re-enactment of the great drama of which he had been part. He managed to infiltrate himself and Laurien into the crowd of extras who were milling about on a life-size model of the *Titanic* constructed in a field in the Pinewood Studios. Unwisely, he pushed his way to the front of the mob of stricken passengers just before the cameras were about to roll and was spotted by the director. Over the megaphone came an invitation for Mr Beesley and his daughter kindly to leave the set immediately.

Laurien dryly recounted this episode in a preface she contributed to a paperback reissue of her father's book. The preface is unusually well written and I suspect may have been edited by a friend of hers, the novelist Julian Barnes. In describing Lawrence's undignified eviction from the set, Laurien (or Julian) wrote, 'And so, for the second time in his life, my father found himself leaving the deck of the *Titanic* in a hurry.'

Lawrence never gave up his interest in spiritual matters. I recall him showing me both his microscope and his Ouija board. He also took up dousing, or water-divining. Even as a boy of fourteen, I was surprised that so many underground torrents apparently coursed beneath his suburban garden, prompting his forked stick to twitch upward every dozen or so steps he took.

Lawrence died on 14 February 1967 at the age of eighty-nine. His book on the *Titanic* is his enduring achievement.

Of his children, Alec died in 1987, three years before Dodie. Of his daughters Dinah and Waveney, the mothers of large and happy families, Dinah is still going strong at the age of 99 but Waveney died in 2011. My mother Laurien died in 2009 after a long illness. Vera, the eldest sister, died in childhood. Hugh was killed in the Second World War after the plane he was flying was lost at sea off the coast of West Africa.

'The pleasures of the joyful heart hang by a single, silken thread,' wrote the Persian poet Hafez. The lives of Lawrence's many descendants hang by a slender strand that could so easily have been broken, his escape against heavy odds from an overwhelming disaster. Here follows his account, as clear and compelling as on the day it was written a century ago.

Nicholas Wade
31 October 2011

I am indebted for many facts and dates given here to Pat Cook of Houston, a *Titanic* expert and author of *The Annotated 'Loss of the SS Titanic'*, a privately printed monograph.

Preface to the 1912 Edition

The circumstances in which this book came to be written are as follows. Some five weeks after the survivors from the *Titanic* landed in New York, I was the guest at luncheon of Hon. Samuel J. Elder and Hon. Charles T. Gallagher, both well-known lawyers in Boston. After luncheon I was asked to relate to those present the experiences of the survivors in leaving the *Titanic* and reaching the *Carpathia*.

When I had done so, Mr Robert Lincoln O'Brien, the editor of the *Boston Herald*, urged me as a matter of public interest to write a correct history of the *Titanic* disaster, his reason being that he knew several publications were in preparation by people who had not been present at the disaster, but from newspaper accounts were piecing together a description of it. He said that these publications would probably be erroneous, full of highly coloured details, and generally calculated to disturb public thought on the matter. He was supported in his request by all present, and under this general pressure I accompanied him to Messrs. Houghton Mifflin Company, where we discussed the question of publication.

Messrs. Houghton Mifflin Company took at that time exactly the same view that I did, that it was probably not advisable to put on record the incidents connected with the *Titanic*'s sinking: it seemed better to forget details as rapidly as possible.

However, we decided to take a few days to think about it. At our next meeting we found ourselves in agreement again – but this time on the common ground that it would probably be a wise thing to write a history of the *Titanic* disaster as correctly as possible. I was supported in this decision by the fact that a short account, which I wrote at intervals on board the *Carpathia*, in the hope that it would calm public opinion by stating the truth of what happened as nearly as I could recollect it, appeared in all the American, English, and Colonial papers and had exactly the effect it was intended to have. This encourages me to hope that the effect of this work will be the same.

Another matter aided me in coming to a decision – the duty that we, as survivors of the disaster, owe to those who went down with the ship, to see that the reforms so urgently needed are not allowed to be forgotten.

Whoever reads the account of the cries that came to us afloat on the sea from those sinking in the ice-cold water must remember that they were addressed to him just as much as to those who heard them, and that the duty, of seeing that reforms are carried out devolves on every one who knows that such cries were heard in utter helplessness the night the *Titanic* sank.

I

Construction and Preparations
for the First Voyage

The history of the RMS *Titanic*, of the White Star Line, is one of the most tragically short it is possible to conceive. The world had waited expectantly for its launching and again for its sailing; had read accounts of its tremendous size and its unexampled completeness and luxury; had felt it a matter of the greatest satisfaction that such a comfortable, and above all such a safe boat had been designed and built – the 'unsinkable lifeboat' – and then in a moment to hear that it had gone to the bottom as if it had been the veriest tramp steamer of a few hundred tons; and with it fifteen hundred passengers, some of them known the world over! The improbability of such a thing ever happening was what staggered humanity.

If its history had to be written in a single paragraph it would be somewhat as follows:

The RMS *Titanic* was built by Messrs. Harland & Wolff at their well-known ship-building works at Queen's Island, Belfast, side by side with her sister ship the *Olympic*. The twin vessels marked such an increase in size that specially laid-out joiner and boiler shops were prepared to aid in their construction, and the space usually taken up by three building slips was given up to them. The keel of the *Titanic* was laid on 31 March 1909, and she was launched on 31 May 1911; she passed her trials before the Board of Trade officials on 31 March 1912, at Belfast, arrived at Southampton on 4 April and sailed the following Wednesday, 10 April with 2,208 passengers and crew, on her maiden voyage to New York. She called at Cherbourg the same day, Queenstown Thursday, and left for New York in the afternoon, expecting to arrive the following Wednesday morning. But the voyage was never completed. She collided with an iceberg on Sunday at 11.45 p.m. in Lat. 41° 46′ N. and Long. 50° 14′ W., and sank two hours and a half later; 815 of her passengers and 688 of her crew were drowned and 705 rescued by the *Carpathia*.

Such is the record of the *Titanic*, the largest ship the world had ever seen – she was three inches longer than the *Olympic* and one thousand tons more in gross tonnage – and her end was the greatest maritime disaster known. The whole civilised world was stirred to its depths when the full extent of loss of life was learned, and it has not yet recovered from the shock. And that is without doubt a good thing. It should not recover from it until the possibility of such a disaster occurring again has been utterly removed from human society, whether by separate legislation in different countries or by international agreement. No living person should seek to dwell in thought for one moment on such a disaster except in the endeavour to glean from it knowledge that will be of profit to the whole world in the future. When such knowledge is practically applied in the construction, equipment, and navigation of passenger steamers – and not until then – will be the time to cease to think of the *Titanic* disaster and of the hundreds of men and women so needlessly sacrificed.

A few words on the ship's construction and equipment will be necessary in order to make clear many points that arise in the course of this book. A few figures have been added which it is hoped will help the reader to follow events more closely than he otherwise could.

The considerations that inspired the builders to design the *Titanic* on the lines on which she was constructed were those of speed, weight of displacement, passenger and cargo accommodation. High speed is very expensive, because the initial cost of the necessary powerful machinery is enormous, the running expenses entailed very heavy, and passenger and cargo accommodation have to be fined down to make the resistance through the water as little as possible and to keep the weight down. An increase in size brings a builder at once into conflict with the question of dock and harbour accommodation at the ports she will touch: if her total displacement is very great while the lines are kept slender for speed, the draught limit may be exceeded. The *Titanic*, therefore, was built on broader lines than the ocean racers, increasing the total displacement; but because of the broader build, she was able to keep within the draught limit at each port she visited. At the same time she was able to accommodate more passengers and cargo, and thereby increase largely her earning capacity. A comparison between the *Mauretania* and the *Titanic* illustrates the difference in these respects:

	Displacement	Horse power	Speed in knots
Mauretania	44,640	70,000	26
Titanic	60,000	46,000	21

The vessel when completed was 883 feet long, 92 $1/2$ feet broad; her height from keel to bridge was 104 feet. She had 8 steel decks, a cellular double bottom, 5 $1/4$ feet through (the inner and outer 'skins' so-called), and with bilge keels projecting 2 feet for 300 feet of her length amidships. These latter were intended to lessen the tendency to roll in a sea; they no doubt did so very well, but, as it happened, they proved to be a weakness, for this was the first portion of the ship touched by the iceberg and it has been suggested that the keels were forced inwards by the collision and made the work of smashing in the two 'skins' a more simple matter. Not that the final result would have been any different.

Her machinery was an expression of the latest progress in marine engineering, being a combination of reciprocating engines with Parsons's low-pressure turbine engine – a combination which gives increased power with the same steam consumption, an advance on the use of reciprocating engines alone. The reciprocating engines drove the wing-propellers and the turbine a mid-propeller, making her a triple-screw vessel. To drive these engines she had 29 enormous boilers and 159 furnaces. Three elliptical funnels, 24 feet 6 inches in the widest diameter, took away smoke and water gases; the fourth one was a dummy for ventilation.

She was fitted with 16 lifeboats 30 feet long, swung on davits of the Welin double-acting type. These davits are specially designed for dealing with two, and, where necessary, three, sets of lifeboats – i.e., 48 altogether; more than enough to have saved every soul on board on the night of the collision. She was divided into 16 compartments by 15 transverse watertight bulkheads reaching from the double bottom to the upper deck in the forward end and to the saloon deck in the after end, in both cases well above the water line. Communication between the engine rooms and boiler rooms was through watertight doors, which could all be closed instantly from the captain's bridge: a single switch, controlling powerful electro-magnets, operated them. They could also be closed by hand with a lever, and in case the floor below them was flooded by accident, a float underneath the flooring shut them automatically. These compartments were so designed that if the two largest were flooded with water – a most unlikely contingency in the ordinary way – the ship would still be quite safe. Of course, more than two were flooded the night of the collision, but exactly how many is not yet thoroughly established.

Her crew had a complement of 860, made up of 475 stewards, cooks, etc., 320 engineers, and 65 engaged in her navigation. The machinery and equipment of the *Titanic* was the finest obtainable and represented the last word in marine construction. All her structure was of steel, of a weight, size, and thickness greater than that of any ship yet known: the girders, beams, bulkheads, and floors all of exceptional strength. It would hardly seem necessary to mention this, were it not that there is an impression among a portion of the general public that the provision of Turkish baths, gymnasiums, and other so-called luxuries involved a sacrifice of some more essential things, the absence of which was responsible for the loss of so many lives. But this is quite an erroneous impression. All these things were an additional provision for the comfort and convenience of passengers, and there is no more reason why they should not be provided on these ships than in a large hotel. There were places on the *Titanic's* deck where more boats and rafts could have been stored without sacrificing these things. The fault lay in not providing them, not in designing the ship without places to put them. On whom the responsibility must rest for their not being provided is another matter and must be left until later.

When arranging a tour round the United States, I had decided to cross in the *Titanic* for several reasons – one, that it was rather a novelty to be on board the largest ship yet launched, and another that friends who had crossed in the *Olympic* described her as a most comfortable boat in a seaway, and it was reported that the *Titanic* had been still further improved in this respect by having a thousand tons more built in to steady her. I went on board at Southampton at 10 a.m. Wednesday 10 April, after staying the night in the town. It is pathetic to recall that as I sat that morning in the breakfast room of a hotel, from the windows of which could be seen the four huge funnels of the *Titanic* towering over the roofs of the various shipping offices opposite, and the procession of stokers and stewards wending their way to the ship, there sat behind me three of the *Titanic's* passengers discussing the coming voyage and estimating, among other things, the probabilities of an accident at sea to the ship. As I rose from breakfast, I glanced at the group and recognised them later on board, but they were not among the number who answered to the roll-call on the *Carpathia* on the following Monday morning.

Between the time of going on board and sailing, I inspected, in the company of two friends who had come from Exeter to see me off, the various decks, dining-saloons and libraries; and so extensive were they that it is no exaggeration to say that it was quite easy to lose one's way on such a ship. We wandered casually into the gymnasium on the boatdeck, and were engaged in bicycle exercise when the instructor came in with two photographers and insisted on our remaining there while his friends – as we thought at the time – made a record for him of his apparatus in use. It was only later that we discovered that they were the photographers of one of the illustrated London papers. More passengers came in, and the instructor ran here and there, looking the very picture of robust, rosy-cheeked health and 'fitness' in his white flannels, placing one passenger on the electric 'horse', another on the 'camel', while the laughing group of onlookers watched the inexperienced riders vigorously shaken up and down as he controlled the little motor which made the machines imitate so realistically horse and camel exercise.

It is related that on the night of the disaster, right up to the time of the *Titanic*'s sinking, while the band grouped outside the gymnasium doors played with such supreme courage in face of the water which rose foot by foot before their eyes, the instructor was on duty inside, with passengers on the bicycles and the rowing-machines, still assisting and encouraging to the last. Along with the bandsmen it is fitting that his name, which I do not think has yet been put on record – it is McCawley – should have a place in the honourable list of those who did their duty faithfully to the ship and the line they served.

2

From Southampton to the Night of the Collision

Soon after noon the whistles blew for friends to go ashore, the gangways were withdrawn, and the *Titanic* moved slowly down the dock, to the accompaniment of last messages and shouted farewells of those on the quay. There was no cheering or hooting of steamers' whistles from the fleet of ships that lined the dock, as might seem probable on the occasion of the largest vessel in the world putting to sea on her maiden voyage; the whole scene was quiet and rather ordinary, with little of the picturesque and interesting ceremonial which imagination paints as usual in such circumstances. But if this was lacking, two unexpected dramatic incidents supplied a thrill of excitement and interest to the departure from dock. The first of these occurred just before the last gangway was withdrawn – a knot of stokers ran along the quay, with their kit slung over their shoulders in bundles, and made for the gangway with the evident intention of joining the ship. But a petty officer guarding the shore end of the gangway firmly refused to allow them on board; they argued, gesticulated, apparently attempting to explain the reasons why they were late, but he remained obdurate and waved them back with a determined hand, the gangway was dragged back amid their protests, putting a summary ending to their determined efforts to join the *Titanic*. Those stokers must be thankful men today that some circumstance, whether their own lack of punctuality or some unforeseen delay over which they had no control, prevented their being in time to run up that last gangway! They will have told – and will no doubt tell for years – the story of how their lives were probably saved by being too late to join the *Titanic*.

The second incident occurred soon afterwards, and while it has no doubt been thoroughly described at the time by those on shore, perhaps a view of the occurrence from the deck of the *Titanic* will not be without interest. As the *Titanic* moved majestically down the dock, the crowd of friends keeping pace with us along the quay, we came together level with the steamer *New York* lying moored to the side of the dock along with the *Oceanic*, the crowd waving 'goodbyes' to those on board as well as they could for the intervening bulk of the two ships. But as the bows of our ship came about level with those of the *New York*, there came a series of reports like those of a revolver, and on the quay side of the *New York* snaky coils of thick rope flung themselves high in the air and fell backwards among the crowd, which retreated in alarm to escape the flying ropes. We hoped that no one was struck by the ropes, but a sailor next to me was certain he saw a woman carried away to receive attention. And then, to our amazement the *New York* crept towards us, slowly and stealthily, as if drawn by some invisible force which she was powerless to withstand. It reminded me instantly of an experiment I had shown many times to a form of boys learning the elements of physics in a laboratory, in which a small magnet is made to float on a cork in a bowl of water and small steel objects placed on neighbouring pieces of cork are drawn up to the floating magnet by magnetic force. It reminded me, too, of seeing in my little boy's bath how a large celluloid floating duck would draw towards itself, by what is called capillary attraction, smaller ducks, frogs, beetles, and other animal folk, until the menagerie floated about as a unit, oblivious of their natural antipathies and reminding us of the 'happy families' one sees in cages on the seashore. On the *New York* there was shouting of orders, sailors running to and fro, paying out ropes and putting mats over the side where it seemed likely we should collide; the tug which had a few moments before cast off from the bows of the *Titanic* came up around our stern and passed to the quay side of the *New York*'s stern, made fast to her and started to haul her back with all the force her engines were capable of; but it did not seem that the tug made much impression on the *New York*. Apart from the serious nature of the accident, it made an irresistibly comic picture to see the huge vessel drifting down the dock with a snorting tug at its heels, for all the world like a small boy dragging a diminutive puppy down the road with its teeth locked on a piece of rope, its feet splayed out, its head and body shaking from side to side in the effort to get every ounce of its weight used to the best advantage. At first all appearance showed that the sterns of the two vessels would collide; but from the stern bridge of the *Titanic* an officer directing operations stopped us dead, the suction ceased, and the *New York* with her tug trailing behind moved obliquely down the dock, her stern gliding along the side of the *Titanic* some few yards away. It gave an extraordinary impression of the absolute helplessness of a big liner in the absence of any motive power to guide her. But all excitement was not yet over: the *New York* turned her bows inward towards the quay, her stern swinging just clear of and passing in front of our bows, and moved slowly head on for the *Teutonic* lying moored to the side; mats were quickly got out and so deadened the force of the collision, which from where we were seemed to be too slight to cause any damage. Another tug came up and took hold of the *New York* by the bows; and between the two of them they dragged her round the corner of the quay which just here came to an end on the side of the river.

We now moved slowly ahead and passed the *Teutonic* at a creeping pace, but notwithstanding this, the latter strained at her ropes so much that she heeled over several degrees in her efforts to follow the *Titanic*: the crowd were shouted back, a group of gold-braided officials, probably the harbour-master and his staff, standing on the sea side of the moored ropes, jumped back over them as they drew up taut to a rigid line, and urged the crowd back still farther. But we were just clear, and as we slowly turned the corner into the river I saw the *Teutonic* swing slowly back into her normal station, relieving the tension alike of the ropes and of the minds of all who witnessed the incident.

Unpleasant as this incident was, it was interesting to all the passengers leaning over the rails to see the means adopted by the officers and crew of the various vessels to avoid collision, to see on the *Titanic*'s docking-bridge (at the stern) an officer and seamen telephoning and ringing bells, hauling up and down little red and white flags, as danger of collision alternately threatened and diminished. No one was more interested than a young American kinematograph photographer, who, with his wife, followed the whole scene with eager eyes, turning the handle of his camera with the most evident pleasure as he recorded the unexpected incident on his films. It was obviously quite a windfall for him to have been on board at such a time. But neither the film nor those who exposed it reached the other side, and the record of the accident from the *Titanic*'s deck has never been thrown on the screen.

As we steamed down the river, the scene we had just witnessed was the topic of every conversation: the comparison with the *Olympic–*

Hawke collision was drawn in every little group of passengers, and it seemed to be generally agreed that this would confirm the suction theory which was so successfully advanced by the cruiser *Hawke* in the law courts, but which many people scoffed at when the British Admiralty first suggested it as the explanation of the cruiser ramming the *Olympic*. And since this is an attempt to chronicle facts as they happened on board the *Titanic*, it must be recorded that there were among the passengers and such of the crew as were heard to speak on the matter, the direst misgivings at the incident we had just witnessed. Sailors are proverbially superstitious; far too many people are prone to follow their lead, or, indeed, the lead of anyone who asserts a statement with an air of conviction and the opportunity of constant repetition; the sense of mystery that shrouds a prophetic utterance, particularly if it be an ominous one (for so constituted apparently is the human mind that it will receive the impress of an evil prophecy far more readily than it will that of a beneficent one, possibly through subservient fear to the thing it dreads, possibly through the degraded, morbid attraction which the sense of evil has for the innate evil in the human mind), leads many people to pay a certain respect to superstitious theories. Not that they wholly believe in them or would wish their dearest friends to know they ever gave them a second thought; but the feeling that other people do so and the half conviction that there 'may be something in it, after all,' sways them into tacit obedience to the most absurd and childish theories. I wish in a later chapter to discuss the subject of superstition in its reference to our life on board the *Titanic*, but will anticipate events here a little by relating a second so-called 'bad omen' which was hatched at Queenstown. As one of the tenders containing passengers and mails neared the *Titanic*, some of those on board gazed up at the liner towering above them, and saw a stoker's head, black from his work in the stokehold below, peering out at them from the top of one of the enormous funnels – a dummy one for ventilation – that rose many feet above the highest deck. He had climbed up inside for a joke, but to some of those who saw him there the sight was seed for the growth of an 'omen', which bore fruit in an unknown dread of dangers to come. An American lady – may she forgive me if she reads these lines! – has related to me with the deepest conviction and earnestness of manner that she saw the man and attributes the sinking of the *Titanic* largely to that. Arrant foolishness, you may say! Yes, indeed, but not to those who believe in it; and it is well not to have such prophetic thoughts of danger passed round among passengers and crew: it would seem to have an unhealthy influence.

We dropped down Spithead, past the shores of the Isle of Wight looking superbly beautiful in new spring foliage, exchanged salutes with a White Star tug lying-to in wait for one of their liners inward bound, and saw in the distance several warships with attendant black destroyers guarding the entrance from the sea. In the calmest weather we made Cherbourg just as it grew dusk and left again about 8.30, after taking on board passengers and mails. We reached Queenstown about 12 noon on Thursday, after a most enjoyable passage across the Channel, although the wind was almost too cold to allow of sitting out on deck on Thursday morning.

The coast of Ireland looked very beautiful as we approached Queenstown Harbour, the brilliant morning sun showing up the green hillsides and picking out groups of dwellings dotted here and there above the rugged grey cliffs that fringed the coast. We took on board our pilot, ran slowly towards the harbour with the sounding-line dropping all the time, and came to a stop well out to sea, with our screws churning up the bottom and turning the sea all brown with sand from below. It had seemed to me that the ship stopped rather suddenly, and in my ignorance of the depth of the harbour entrance, that perhaps the sounding-line had revealed a smaller depth than was thought safe for the great size of the *Titanic*: this seemed to be confirmed by the sight of sand churned up from the bottom – but this is mere supposition. Passengers and mails were put on board from two tenders, and nothing could have given us a better idea of the enormous length and bulk of the *Titanic* than to stand as far astern as possible and look over the side from the top deck, forwards and downwards to where the tenders rolled at her bows, the merest cockleshells beside the majestic vessel that rose deck after deck above them. Truly she was a magnificent boat! There was something so graceful in her movement as she rode up and down on the slight swell in the harbour, a slow, stately dip and recover, only noticeable by watching her bows in comparison with some landmark on the coast in the near distance; the two little tenders tossing up and down like corks beside her illustrated vividly the advance made in comfort of motion from the time of the small steamer.

Presently the work of transfer was ended, the tenders cast off, and at 1.30 p.m., with the screws churning up the sea bottom again, the *Titanic* turned slowly through a quarter-circle until her nose pointed down along the Irish coast, and then steamed rapidly away from Queenstown, the little house on the left of the town gleaming white on the hillside for many miles astern. In our wake soared and screamed hundreds of gulls, which had quarrelled and fought over the remnants of lunch pouring out of the waste pipes as we lay-to in the harbour entrance; and now they followed us in the expectation of further spoil. I watched them for a long time and was astonished at the ease with which they soared and kept up with the ship with hardly a motion of their wings: picking out a particular gull, I would keep him under observation for minutes at a time and see no motion of his wings downwards or upwards to aid his flight. He would tilt all of a piece to one side or another as the gusts of wind caught him: rigidly unbendable, as an aeroplane tilts sideways in a puff of wind. And yet with graceful ease he kept pace with the *Titanic* forging through the water at twenty knots: as the wind met him he would rise upwards and obliquely forwards, and come down slantingly again, his wings curved in a beautiful arch and his tail feathers outspread as a fan. It was plain that he was possessed of a secret we are only just beginning to learn – that of utilising air-currents as escalators up and down which he can glide at will with the expenditure of the minimum amount of energy, or of using them as a ship does when it sails within one or two points of a head wind. Aviators, of course, are imitating the gull, and soon perhaps we may see an aeroplane or a glider dipping gracefully up and down in the face of an opposing wind and all the time forging ahead across the Atlantic Ocean. The gulls were still behind us when night fell, and still they screamed and dipped down into the broad wake of foam which we left behind; but in the morning they were gone: perhaps they had seen in the night a steamer bound for their Queenstown home and had escorted her back.

All afternoon we steamed along the coast of Ireland, with grey cliffs guarding the shores, and hills rising behind gaunt and barren; as dusk fell, the coast rounded away from us to the north-west, and the last we saw of Europe was the Irish mountains dim and faint in the dropping darkness. With the thought that we had seen the last of land until we set foot on the shores of America, I retired to the library to write letters, little knowing that many things would happen to us all – many experiences, sudden, vivid and impressive to be encountered, many perils to be faced, many good and true people for whom we should have to mourn – before we saw land again.

There is very little to relate from the time of leaving Queenstown on Thursday to Sunday morning. The sea was calm – so calm, indeed, that very few were absent from meals: the wind westerly and south-westerly – 'fresh' as the daily chart described it – but often rather cold, generally too cold to sit out on deck to read or write, so that many of us spent a good part of the time in the library, reading and writing. I wrote a large number of letters and posted them day by day in the box outside the library door: possibly they are there yet.

Each morning the sun rose behind us in a sky of circular clouds, stretching round the horizon in long, narrow streaks and rising tier upon tier above the skyline, red and pink and fading from pink to white, as the sun rose higher in the sky. It was a beautiful sight to one who had not crossed the ocean before (or indeed been out of sight of the shores of England) to stand on the top deck and watch the swell of the sea extending outwards from the ship in an unbroken circle until it met the skyline with its hint of infinity: behind, the wake of the vessel white with foam where, fancy suggested, the propeller blades had cut up the long Atlantic rollers and with them made a level white road bounded on either side by banks of green, blue, and blue-green waves that would presently sweep away the white road, though as yet it stretched back to the horizon and dipped over the edge of the world back to Ireland and the gulls, while along it the morning sun glittered and sparkled. And each night the sun sank right in our eyes along the sea, making an undulating glittering pathway, a golden track charted on the surface of the ocean which our ship followed unswervingly until the sun dipped below the edge of the horizon, and the pathway ran ahead of us faster than we could steam and slipped over the edge of the skyline – as if the sun had been a golden ball and had wound up its thread of gold too quickly for us to follow.

From 12 noon Thursday to 12 noon Friday we ran 386 miles, Friday to Saturday 519 miles, Saturday to Sunday 546 miles. The second day's run of 519 miles was, the purser told us, a disappointment, and we should not dock until Wednesday morning instead of Tuesday night, as we had expected; however, on Sunday we were glad to see a longer run had been made, and it was thought we should make New York, after all, on Tuesday night. The purser remarked: 'They are not pushing her this trip and don't intend to make any fast running: I don't suppose we shall do more than 546 now; it is not a bad day's run for the first trip.' This was at lunch, and I remember the conversation then turned to the speed and build of Atlantic liners as factors in their comfort of motion: all those who had crossed many times were unanimous in saying the *Titanic* was the most comfortable boat they had been on, and they preferred the speed we were making to that of the faster boats, from the point of view of lessened vibration as well as because the faster boats would bore through the waves with a twisted, screw-like motion instead of the straight up-and-down swing of the *Titanic*. I then called the attention of our table to the way the *Titanic* listed to port (I had noticed this before), and we all watched the skyline through the portholes as we sat at the purser's table in the saloon: it was plain she did so, for the skyline and sea on the port side were visible most of the time and on the starboard only sky. The purser remarked that probably coal had been used mostly from the starboard side. It is no doubt a common occurrence for all vessels to list to some degree; but in view of the fact that the *Titanic* was cut open on the starboard side and before she sank listed so much to port that there was quite a chasm between her and the swinging lifeboats, across which ladies had to be thrown or to cross on chairs laid flat, the previous listing to port may be of interest.

Returning for a moment to the motion of the *Titanic*, it was interesting to stand on the boat deck, as I frequently did, in the angle between lifeboats 13 and 15 on the starboard side (two boats I have every reason to remember, for the first carried me in safety to the *Carpathia*, and it seemed likely at one time that the other would come down on our heads as we sat in 13 trying to get away from the ship's side), and watch the general motion of the ship through the waves resolve itself into two motions – one to be observed by contrasting the docking-bridge, from which the log-line trailed away behind in the foaming wake, with the horizon, and observing the long, slow heave as we rode up and down. I timed the average period occupied in one up-and-down vibration, but do not now remember the figures. The second motion was a side-to-side roll, and could be calculated by watching the port rail and contrasting it with the horizon as before. It seems likely that this double motion is due to the angle at which our direction to New York cuts the general set of the Gulf Stream sweeping from the Gulf of Mexico across to Europe; but the almost clock-like regularity of the two vibratory movements was what attracted my attention: it was while watching the side roll that I first became aware of the list to port. Looking down astern from the boat deck or from B deck to the steerage quarters, I often noticed how the third class passengers were enjoying every minute of the time: a most uproarious skipping game of the mixed-double type was the great favourite, while 'in and out and roundabout' went a Scotchman with his bagpipes playing something that Gilbert says 'faintly resembled an air'. Standing aloof from all of them, generally on the raised stern deck above the 'playing field', was a man of about twenty to twenty-four years of age, well-dressed, always gloved and nicely groomed, and obviously quite out of place among his fellow passengers: he never looked happy all the time. I watched him, and classified him at hazard as the man who had been a failure in some way at home and had received the proverbial shilling plus third class fare to America: he did not look resolute enough or happy enough to be working out his own problem. Another interesting man was travelling steerage, but had placed his wife in the second cabin: he would climb the stairs leading from the steerage to the second deck and talk affectionately with his wife across the low gate which separated them. I never saw him after the collision, but I think his wife was on the *Carpathia*. Whether they ever saw each other on the Sunday night is very doubtful: he would not at first be allowed on the second class deck, and if he were, the chances of seeing his wife in the darkness and the crowd would be very small, indeed. Of all those playing so happily on the steerage deck I did not recognise many afterwards on the *Carpathia*.

Coming now to Sunday, the day on which the *Titanic* struck the iceberg, it will be interesting, perhaps, to give the day's events in some detail, to appreciate the general attitude of passengers to their surroundings just before the collision. Service was held in the saloon by the purser in the morning, and going on deck after lunch we found such a change in temperature that not many cared to remain to face the bitter wind – an artificial wind created mainly, if not entirely, by the ship's rapid motion through the chilly atmosphere. I should judge there was no wind blowing at the time, for I had noticed about the same force of wind approaching Queenstown, to find that it died away as soon as we stopped, only to rise again as we steamed away from the harbour.

Returning to the library, I stopped for a moment to read again the day's run and observe our position on the chart; the Rev. Mr Carter, a clergyman of the Church of England, was similarly engaged, and we renewed a conversation we had enjoyed for some days: it had commenced with a discussion of the relative merits of his university – Oxford – with mine – Cambridge – as world-wide educational agencies, the opportunities at each for the formation of character apart from mere education as such, and had led on to the lack of sufficiently qualified men to take up the work of the Church of England (a matter apparently on which he felt very deeply) and from that to his own work in England as a priest. He told me some of his parish problems and spoke of the impossibility of doing half his work in his church without the help his wife gave. I knew her only slightly at that time, but meeting her later in the day, I realised something of what he meant in attributing a large part of what success he had as a vicar to her. My only excuse for mentioning these details about the Carters – now and later in the day – is that, while they have perhaps not much interest for the average reader, they will no doubt be some comfort to the parish over which he presided and where I am sure he was loved. He next mentioned the absence of a service in the evening and asked if I knew the purser well enough to request the use of the saloon in the evening where he would like to have a 'hymn sing-song'; the purser gave his consent at once, and Mr Carter made preparations during the afternoon by asking all he knew – and many he did not – to come to the saloon at 8.30 p.m.

The library was crowded that afternoon, owing to the cold on deck, but through the windows we could see the clear sky with brilliant sunlight that seemed to augur a fine night and a clear day tomorrow, and the prospect of landing in two days, with calm weather all the way to New York, was a matter of general satisfaction among us all. I can look back and see every detail of the library that afternoon – the beautifully furnished room, with lounges, armchairs, and small writing- or card-tables scattered about, writing-bureaus round the walls of the room, and the library in glass-cased shelves flanking one side, – the whole finished in mahogany relieved with white fluted wooden columns that supported the deck above. Through the windows there is the covered corridor, reserved by general consent as the children's playground, and here are playing the two Navatril children with their father – devoted to them, never absent from them. Who would have thought of the dramatic history of the happy group at play in the corridor that afternoon! The abduction of the children in Nice, the assumed name, the separation of father and children in a few hours, his death and their subsequent union with their mother after a period of doubt as to their parentage! How many more similar secrets the *Titanic* revealed in the privacy of family life, or carried down with her untold, we shall never know.

In the same corridor is a man and his wife with two children, and one of them he is generally carrying: they are all young and happy: he is dressed always in a grey knickerbocker suit – with a camera slung over his shoulder. I have not seen any of them since that afternoon.

Close beside me – so near that I cannot avoid hearing scraps of their conversation – are two American ladies, both dressed in white, young, probably friends only: one has been to India and is returning by way of England, the other is a school teacher in America, a graceful girl with a distinguished air heightened by a pair of *pince-nez*. Engaged in conversation with them is a gentleman whom I subsequently identified from a photograph as a well-known resident of Cambridge, Massachusetts, genial, polished, and with a courtly air towards the two ladies, whom he has known but a few hours; from time to time as they talk, a child acquaintance breaks in on their conversation and insists on their taking notice of a large doll clasped in her arms; I have seen none of this group since then. In the opposite corner are the young American kinematograph photographer and his young wife, evidently French, very fond of playing patience, which she is doing now, while he sits back in his chair watching the game and interposing from time to time with suggestions. I did not see them again. In the middle of the room are two Catholic priests, one quietly reading – either English or Irish, and probably the latter – the other, dark, bearded, with broad-brimmed hat, talking earnestly to a friend in German and evidently explaining some verse in the open Bible before him; near them a young fire engineer on his way to Mexico, and of the same religion as the rest of the group. None of them were saved. It may be noted here that the percentage of men saved in the second class is the lowest of any other division – only 8 per cent.

Many other faces recur to thought, but it is impossible to describe them all in the space of a short book: of all those in the library that Sunday afternoon, I can remember only two or three persons who found their way to the *Carpathia*. Looking over this room, with his back to the library shelves, is the library steward, thin, stooping, sad-faced, and generally with nothing to do but serve out books; but this afternoon he is busier than I have ever seen him, serving out baggage declaration forms for passengers to fill in. Mine is before me as I write: 'Form for nonresidents in the United States. Steamship *Titanic*: No. 31444, D,' etc. I had filled it in that afternoon and slipped it in my pocketbook instead of returning it to the steward. Before me, too, is a small cardboard square: 'White Star Line. RMS *Titanic*. 208. This label must be given up when the article is returned. The property will be deposited in the Purser's safe. The Company will not be liable to passengers for the loss of money, jewels, or ornaments, by theft or otherwise, not so deposited.' The 'property deposited' in my case was money, placed in an envelope, sealed, with my name written across the flap, and handed to the purser; the 'label' is my receipt. Along with other similar envelopes it may be still intact in the safe at the bottom of the sea, but in all probability it is not, as will be seen presently.

After dinner, Mr Carter invited all who wished to the saloon, and with the assistance at the piano of a gentleman who sat at the purser's table opposite me (a young Scotch engineer going out to join his brother fruit-farming at the foot of the Rockies), he started some hundred passengers singing hymns. They were asked to choose whichever hymn they wished, and with so many to choose, it was impossible for him to do more than have the greatest favourites sung. As he announced each hymn, it was evident that he was thoroughly versed in their history: no hymn was sung but that he gave a short sketch of its author and in some cases a description of the circumstances in which it was composed. I think all were impressed with his knowledge of hymns and with his eagerness to tell us all he knew of them. It was curious to see how many chose hymns dealing with dangers at sea. I noticed the hushed tone with which all sang the hymn 'For those in peril on the Sea'.

The singing must have gone on until after ten o'clock, when, seeing the stewards standing about waiting to serve biscuits and coffee before going off duty, Mr Carter brought the evening to a close by a few words of thanks to the purser for the use of the saloon, a short sketch of the happiness and safety of the voyage hitherto, the great confidence all felt on board this great liner with her steadiness and her size, and the happy outlook of landing in a few hours in New York at the close of a delightful voyage; and all the time he spoke, a few miles ahead of us lay the 'peril on the sea' that was to sink this same great liner with many of those on board who listened with gratitude to his simple, heartfelt words. So much for the frailty of human hopes and for the confidence reposed in material human designs.

Think of the shame of it, that a mass of ice of no use to anyone or anything should have the power fatally to injure the beautiful *Titanic*! That an insensible block should be able to threaten, even in the smallest degree, the lives of many good men and women who think and plan and hope and love – and not only to threaten, but to end their lives. It is unbearable! Are we never to educate ourselves to foresee such dangers and to prevent them before they happen? All the evidence of history shows that laws unknown and unsuspected are being discovered day by day: as this knowledge accumulates for the use of man, is it not certain that the ability to see and destroy beforehand the threat of danger will be one of the privileges the whole world will utilise? May that day come soon. Until it does, no precaution too rigorous can be taken, no safety appliance, however costly, must be omitted from a ship's equipment.

After the meeting had broken up, I talked with the Carters over a cup of coffee, said goodnight to them, and retired to my cabin at about quarter to eleven. They were good people and this world is much poorer by their loss.

It may be a matter of pleasure to many people to know that their friends were perhaps among that gathering of people in the saloon, and that at the last the sound of the hymns still echoed in their ears as they stood on the deck so quietly and courageously. Who can tell how much it had to do with the demeanour of some of them and the example this would set to others?

3

The Collision and Embarkation in Lifeboats

I had been fortunate enough to secure a two-berth cabin to myself – D 56 – quite close to the saloon and most convenient in every way for getting about the ship; and on a big ship like the *Titanic* it was quite a consideration to be on D deck, only three decks below the top or boat deck. Below D again were cabins on E and F decks, and to walk from a cabin on F up to the top deck, climbing five flights of stairs on the way, was certainly a considerable task for those not able to take much exercise. The *Titanic* management has been criticised, among other things, for supplying the boat with lifts: it has been said they were an expensive luxury and the room they took up might have been utilised in some way for more life-saving appliances. Whatever else may have been superfluous, lifts certainly were not: old ladies, for example, in cabins on F deck, would hardly have got to the top deck during the whole voyage had they not been able to ring for the lift-boy. Perhaps nothing gave one a greater impression of the size of the ship than to take the lift from the top and drop slowly down past the different floors, discharging and taking in passengers just as in a large hotel. I wonder where the lift-boy was that night. I would have been glad to find him in our boat, or on the *Carpathia* when we took count of the saved. He was quite young – not more than sixteen, I think – a bright-eyed, handsome boy, with a love for the sea and the games on deck and the view over the ocean – and he did not get any of them. One day, as he put me out of his lift and saw through the vestibule windows a game of deck quoits in progress, he said, in a wistful tone, 'My! I wish I could go out there sometimes!' I wished he could, too, and made a jesting offer to take charge of his lift for an hour while he went out to watch the game; but he smilingly shook his head and dropped down in answer to an imperative ring from below. I think he was not on duty with his lift after the collision, but if he were, he would smile at his passengers all the time as he took them up to the boats waiting to leave the sinking ship.

After undressing and climbing into the top berth, I read from about quarter past eleven to the time we struck, about quarter to twelve. During this time I noticed particularly the increased vibration of the ship, and I assumed that we were going at a higher speed than at any other time since we sailed from Queenstown. Now I am aware that this is an important point, and bears strongly on the question of responsibility for the effects of the collision; but the impression of increased vibration is fixed in my memory so strongly that it seems important to record it. Two things led me to this conclusion – first, that as I sat on the sofa undressing, with bare feet on the floor, the jar of the vibration came up from the engines below very noticeably; and second, that as I sat up in the berth reading, the spring mattress supporting me was vibrating more rapidly than usual: this cradle-like motion was always noticeable as one lay in bed, but that night there was certainly a marked increase in the motion. Referring to the plan, it will be seen that the vibration must have come almost directly up from below, when it is mentioned that the saloon was immediately above the engines as shown in the plan, and my cabin next to the saloon. From these two data, on the assumption that greater vibration is an indication of higher speed – and I suppose it must be – then I am sure we were going faster that night at the time we struck the iceberg than we had done before, i.e., during the hours I was awake and able to take note of anything.

And then, as I read in the quietness of the night, broken only by the muffled sound that came to me through the ventilators of stewards talking and moving along the corridors, when nearly all the passengers were in their cabins, some asleep in bed, others undressing, and others only just down from the smoking room and still discussing many things, there came what seemed to me nothing more than an extra heave of the engines and a more than usually obvious dancing motion of the mattress on which I sat. Nothing more than that – no sound of a crash or of anything else: no sense of shock, no jar that felt like one heavy body meeting another. And presently the same thing repeated with about the same intensity. The thought came to me that they must have still further increased the speed. And all this time the *Titanic* was being cut open by the iceberg and water was pouring in her side, and yet no evidence that would indicate such a disaster had been presented to us. It fills me with astonishment now to think of it. Consider the question of list alone. Here was this enormous vessel running starboard-side on to an iceberg, and a passenger sitting quietly in bed, reading, felt no motion or list to the opposite or port side, and this must have been felt had it been more than the usual roll of the ship – never very much in the calm weather we had all the way. Again, my bunk was fixed to the wall on the starboard side, and any list to port would have tended to fling me out on the floor: I am sure I should have noted it had there been any. And yet the explanation is simple enough: the *Titanic* struck the berg with a force of impact of over a million foot-tons; her plates were less than an inch thick, and they must have been cut through as a knife cuts paper: there would be no need to list; it would have been better if she had listed and thrown us out on the floor, for it would have been an indication that our plates were strong enough to offer, at any rate, some resistance to the blow, and we might all have been safe today.

And so, with no thought of anything serious having happened to the ship, I continued my reading; and still the murmur from the stewards and from adjoining cabins, and no other sound: no cry in the night; no alarm given; no one afraid – there was then nothing which could cause fear to the most timid person. But in a few moments I felt the engines slow and stop; the dancing motion and the vibration ceased suddenly after being part of our very existence for four days, and that was the first hint that anything out of the ordinary had happened. We have all 'heard' a loud-ticking clock stop suddenly in a quiet room, and then have noticed the clock and the ticking noise, of which we seemed until then quite unconscious. So in the same way the fact was suddenly brought home to all in the ship that the engines – that part of the ship that drove us through the sea – had stopped dead. But the stopping of the engines gave us no information: we had to make our own calculations as to why we had stopped. Like a flash it came to me: 'We have dropped a propeller blade: when this happens the engines always race away until they are controlled, and this accounts for the extra heave they gave'; not a very logical conclusion when considered now, for the engines should have continued to heave all the time until we stopped, but it was at the time a sufficiently tenable hypothesis to hold. Acting on it, I jumped out of bed, slipped on a dressing gown over pyjamas, put on shoes, and went out of my cabin into the hall near the saloon. Here was a steward leaning against the staircase, probably waiting until those in the smoke room above had gone to bed and he could put out the lights. I said, 'Why have we stopped?' 'I don't know, sir,' he replied, 'but I don't suppose it is anything much.' 'Well,' I said, 'I am going on deck to see what it is,' and started towards the stairs. He smiled indulgently at me as I passed him, and said, 'All right, sir, but it is mighty cold up there.' I am sure at that time he thought I was rather foolish to go up with so little reason, and I must confess I felt rather absurd for not remaining in the cabin: it seemed like making a needless fuss to walk about the ship in a dressing gown. But it was my first trip across the sea; I had enjoyed every minute of it and was keenly alive to note every new experience; and certainly to stop in the middle of the sea with a propeller dropped seemed sufficient reason for going on deck. And yet the steward, with his fatherly smile, and the fact that no one else was about the passages or going upstairs to reconnoitre, made me feel guilty in an undefined way of breaking some code of a ship's regime – an Englishman's fear of being thought 'unusual', perhaps!

I climbed the three flights of stairs, opened the vestibule door leading to the top deck, and stepped out into an atmosphere that cut me, clad as I was, like a knife. Walking to the starboard side, I peered over and saw the sea many feet below, calm and black; forward, the deserted deck stretching away to the first class quarters and the captain's bridge; and behind, the steerage quarters and the stern bridge; nothing more: no iceberg on either side or astern as far as we could see in the darkness. There were two or three men on deck, and with one – the Scotch engineer who played hymns in the saloon – I compared notes of our experiences. He had just begun to undress when the engines stopped and had come up at once, so that he was fairly well-clad; none of us could see anything, and all being quiet and still, the Scotchman and I went down to the next deck. Through the windows of the smoking room we saw a game of cards going on, with several onlookers, and went in to enquire if they knew more than we did. They had apparently felt rather more of the heaving motion, but so far as I remember, none of them had gone out on deck to make any enquiries, even when one of them had seen through the windows an iceberg go by towering above the decks. He had called their attention to it, and they all watched it disappear, but had then at once resumed the game. We asked them the height of the berg and some said one hundred feet, others, sixty feet; one of the onlookers – a motor engineer travelling to America with a model carburetter (he had filled in his declaration form near me in the afternoon and had questioned the library steward how he should declare his patent) – said, 'Well, I am accustomed to estimating distances and I put it at between eighty and ninety feet.' We accepted his estimate and made guesses as to what had happened to the *Titanic*: the general impression was that we had just scraped the iceberg with a glancing blow on the starboard side, and they had stopped as a wise precaution, to examine her thoroughly all over. 'I expect the iceberg has scratched off some of her new paint,' said one, 'and the captain doesn't like to go on until she is painted up again.' We laughed at his estimate of the captain's care for the ship. Poor Captain Smith! – he knew by this time only too well what had happened.

One of the players, pointing to his glass of whiskey standing at his elbow, and turning to an onlooker, said, 'Just run along the deck and see if any ice has come aboard: I would like some for this.' Amid the general laughter at what we thought was his imagination – only too realistic, alas! for when he spoke the forward deck was covered with ice that had tumbled over – and seeing that no more information was forthcoming, I left the smoking room and went down to my cabin, where I sat for some time reading again. I am filled with sorrow to think I never saw any of the occupants of that smoking room again: nearly all young men full of hope for their prospects in a new world; mostly unmarried; keen, alert, with the makings of good citizens. Presently, hearing people walking about the corridors, I looked out and saw several standing in the hall talking to a steward – most of them ladies in dressing gowns; other people were going upstairs, and I decided to go on deck again, but as it was too cold to do so in a dressing gown, I dressed in a Norfolk jacket and trousers and walked up. There were now more people looking over the side and walking about, questioning each other as to why we had stopped, but without obtaining any definite information. I stayed on deck some minutes, walking about vigorously to keep warm and occasionally looking downwards to the sea as if something there would indicate the reason for delay. The ship had now resumed her course, moving very slowly through the water with a little white line of foam on each side. I think we were all glad to see this: it seemed better than standing still. I soon decided to go down again, and as I crossed from the starboard to the port side to go down by the vestibule door, I saw an officer climb on the last lifeboat on the port side – number 16 – and begin to throw off the cover, but I do not remember that anyone paid any particular attention to him. Certainly no one thought they were preparing to man the lifeboats and embark from the ship. All this time there was no apprehension of any danger in the minds of passengers, and no one was in any condition of panic or hysteria; after all, it would have been strange if they had been, without any definite evidence of danger.

As I passed to the door to go down, I looked forward again and saw to my surprise an undoubted tilt downwards from the stern to the bows: only a slight slope, which I don't think anyone had noticed – at any rate, they had not remarked on it. As I went downstairs a confirmation of this tilting forward came in something unusual about

45

the stairs, a curious sense of something out of balance and of not being able to put one's feet down in the right place: naturally, being tilted forward, the stairs would slope downwards at an angle and tend to throw one forward. I could not see any visible slope of the stairway: it was perceptible only by the sense of balance at this time.

On D deck were three ladies – I think they were all saved, and it is a good thing at least to be able to chronicle meeting someone who was saved after so much record of those who were not – standing in the passage near the cabin. 'Oh! why have we stopped?' they said. 'We did stop,' I replied, 'but we are now going on again.' 'Oh, no,' one replied; 'I cannot feel the engines as I usually do, or hear them. Listen!' We listened, and there was no throb audible. Having noticed that the vibration of the engines is most noticeable lying in a bath, where the throb comes straight from the floor through its metal sides – too much so ordinarily for one to put one's head back with comfort on the bath, – I took them along the corridor to a bathroom and made them put their hands on the side of the bath: they were much reassured to feel the engines throbbing down below and to know we were making some headway. I left them and on the way to my cabin passed some stewards standing unconcernedly against the walls of the saloon: one of them, the library steward again, was leaning over a table, writing. It is no exaggeration to say that they had neither any knowledge of the accident nor any feeling of alarm that we had stopped and had not yet gone on again full speed: their whole attitude expressed perfect confidence in the ship and officers.

Turning into my gangway (my cabin being the first in the gangway), I saw a man standing at the other end of it fastening his tie. 'Anything fresh?' he said. 'Not much,' I replied; 'we are going ahead slowly and she is down a little at the bows, but I don't think it is anything serious.' 'Come in and look at this man,' he laughed;

'he won't get up.' I looked in, and in the top bunk lay a man with his back to me, closely wrapped in his bedclothes and only the back of his head visible. 'Why won't he get up? Is he asleep?' I said. 'No,' laughed the man dressing, 'he says –'. But before he could finish the sentence the man above grunted: 'You don't catch me leaving a warm bed to go up on that cold deck at midnight. I know better than that.' We both told him laughingly why he had better get up, but he was certain he was just as safe there and all this dressing was quite unnecessary; so I left them and went again to my cabin. I put on some underclothing, sat on the sofa, and read for some ten minutes, when I heard through the open door, above, the noise of people passing up and down, and a loud shout from above: 'All passengers on deck with lifebelts on.'

I placed the two books I was reading in the side pockets of my Norfolk jacket, picked up my lifebelt (curiously enough, I had taken it down for the first time that night from the wardrobe when I first retired to my cabin) and my dressing gown, and walked upstairs tying on the lifebelt. As I came out of my cabin, I remember seeing the purser's assistant, with his foot on the stairs about to climb them, whisper to a steward and jerk his head significantly behind him; not that I thought anything of it at the time, but I have no doubt he was telling him what had happened up in the bows, and was giving him orders to call all passengers.

Going upstairs with other passengers – no one ran a step or seemed alarmed – we met two ladies coming down: one seized me by the arm and said, 'Oh! I have no lifebelt; will you come down to my cabin and help me to find it?' I returned with them to F deck – the lady who had addressed me holding my arm all the time in a vice-like grip, much to my amusement – and we found a steward in her gangway who took them in and found their lifebelts. Coming upstairs again, I passed the purser's window on F deck, and noticed a light inside; when halfway up to E deck, I heard the heavy metallic clang of the safe door, followed by a hasty step retreating along the corridor towards the first class quarters. I have little doubt it was the purser, who had taken all valuables from his safe and was transferring them to the charge of the first class purser, in the hope they might all be saved in one package. That is why I said above that perhaps the envelope containing my money was not in the safe at the bottom of the sea: it is probably in a bundle, with many others like it, waterlogged at the bottom.

Reaching the top deck, we found many people assembled there, – some fully dressed, with coats and wraps, well-prepared for anything that might happen; others who had thrown wraps hastily round them when they were called or heard the summons to equip themselves with lifebelts – not in much condition to face the cold of that night. Fortunately there was no wind to beat the cold air through our clothing: even the breeze caused by the ship's motion had died entirely away, for the engines had stopped again and the *Titanic* lay peacefully on the surface of the sea – motionless, quiet, not even rocking to the roll of the sea; indeed, as we were to discover presently, the sea was as calm as an inland lake save for the gentle swell which could impart no motion to a ship the size of the *Titanic*. To stand on the deck many feet above the water lapping idly against her sides, and looking much farther off than it really was because of the darkness, gave one a sense of wonderful security: to feel her so steady and still was like standing on a large rock in the middle of the ocean. But there were now more evidences of the coming catastrophe to the observer than had been apparent when on deck last: one was the roar and hiss of escaping steam from the boilers, issuing out of a large steam pipe reaching high up one of the funnels: a harsh, deafening boom that made conversation difficult and no doubt increased the apprehension of some people merely because of the volume of noise: if one imagines twenty locomotives blowing off steam in a low key it would give some idea of the unpleasant sound that met us as we climbed out on the top deck.

But after all it was the kind of phenomenon we ought to expect: engines blow off steam when standing in a station, and why should not a ship's boilers do the same when the ship is not moving? I never heard anyone connect this noise with the danger of boiler explosion, in the event of the ship sinking with her boilers under a high pressure of steam, which was no doubt the true explanation of this precaution. But this is perhaps speculation; some people may have known it quite well, for from the time we came on deck until boat 13 got away, I heard very little conversation of any kind among the passengers. It is not the slightest exaggeration to say that no signs of alarm were exhibited by anyone: there was no indication of panic or hysteria; no cries of fear, and no running to and fro to discover what was the matter, why we had been summoned on deck with lifebelts, and what was to be done with us now we were there. We stood there quietly looking on at the work of the crew as they manned the lifeboats, and no one ventured to interfere with them or offered to help them. It was plain we should be of no use; and the crowd of men and women stood quietly on the deck or paced slowly up and down waiting for orders from the officers.

Now, before we consider any further the events that followed, the state of mind of passengers at this juncture, and the motives which led each one to act as he or she did in the circumstances, it is important to keep in thought the amount of information at our disposal. Men and women act according to judgement based on knowledge of the conditions around them, and the best way to understand some apparently inconceivable things that happened is for anyone to imagine himself or herself standing on deck that night. It seems a mystery to some people that women refused to leave the ship, that some persons retired to their cabins, and so on; but it is a matter of judgement, after all.

So that if the reader will come and stand with the crowd on deck, he must first rid himself entirely of the knowledge that the *Titanic* has sunk – an important necessity, for he cannot see conditions as they existed there through the mental haze arising from knowledge of the greatest maritime tragedy the world has known: he must get rid of any foreknowledge of disaster to appreciate why people acted as they did. Secondly, he had better get rid of any picture in thought painted either by his own imagination or by some artist, whether pictorial or verbal, 'from information supplied'. Some are most inaccurate (these, mostly word-pictures), and where they err, they err on the highly dramatic side. They need not have done so: the whole conditions were dramatic enough in all their bare simplicity, without the addition of any high colouring.

Having made these mental erasures, he will find himself as one of the crowd faced with the following conditions: a perfectly still atmosphere; a brilliantly beautiful starlight night, but no moon, and so with little light that was of any use; a ship that had come quietly to rest without any indication of disaster – no iceberg visible, no hole in the ship's side through which water was pouring in, nothing broken or out of place, no sound of alarm, no panic, no movement of anyone except at a walking pace; the absence of any knowledge of the nature of the accident, of the extent of damage, of the danger of the ship sinking in a few hours, of the numbers of boats, rafts, and other lifesaving appliances available, their capacity, what other ships were near or coming to help – in fact, an almost complete absence of any positive knowledge on any point. I think this was the result of deliberate judgement on the part of the officers, and perhaps it was the best thing that could be done. In particular, he must remember that the ship was a sixth of a mile long, with passengers on three decks open to the sea, and port and starboard sides to each deck: he will then get some idea of the difficulty presented to the officers of keeping control over such a large area, and the impossibility of anyone knowing what was happening except in his own immediate vicinity. Perhaps the whole thing can be summed up best by saying that, after we had embarked in the lifeboats and rowed away from the *Titanic*, it would not have surprised us to hear that all passengers would be saved: the cries of drowning people after the *Titanic* gave the final plunge were a thunderbolt to us. I am aware that the experiences of many of those saved differed in some respects from the above: some had knowledge of certain things, some were experienced travellers and sailors, and therefore deduced more rapidly what was likely to happen; but I think the above gives a fairly accurate representation of the state of mind of most of those on deck that night.

All this time people were pouring up from the stairs and adding to the crowd: I remember at that moment thinking it would be well to return to my cabin and rescue some money and warmer clothing if we were to embark in boats, but looking through the vestibule windows and seeing people still coming upstairs, I decided it would only cause confusion passing them on the stairs, and so remained on deck.

I was now on the starboard side of the top boat deck; the time about 12.20. We watched the crew at work on the lifeboats, numbers 9, 11, 13, 15, some inside arranging the oars, some coiling ropes on the deck – the ropes which ran through the pulleys to lower to the sea – others with cranks fitted to the rocking arms of the davits. As we watched, the cranks were turned, the davits swung outwards until the boats hung clear of the edge of the deck. Just then an officer came along from the first class deck and shouted above the noise of escaping steam, 'All women and children get down to deck below and all men stand back from the boats.' He had apparently been off duty when the ship struck, and was lightly dressed, with a white muffler twisted hastily round his neck. The men fell back and the women retired below to get into the boats from the next deck. Two women refused at first to leave their husbands, but partly by persuasion and partly by force they were separated from them and sent down to the next deck. I think that by this time the work on the lifeboats and the separation of men and women impressed on us slowly the presence of imminent danger, but it made no difference in the attitude of the crowd: they were just as prepared to obey orders and to do what came next as when they first came on deck. I do not mean that they actually reasoned it out: they were the average Teutonic crowd, with an inborn respect for law and order and for traditions bequeathed to them by generations of ancestors: the reasons that made them act as they did were impersonal, instinctive, hereditary.

But if there were anyone who had not by now realised that the ship was in danger, all doubt on this point was to be set at rest in a dramatic manner. Suddenly a rush of light from the forward deck, a hissing roar that made us all turn from watching the boats, and a rocket leapt upwards to where the stars blinked and twinkled above us. Up it went, higher and higher, with a sea of faces upturned to watch it, and then an explosion that seemed to split the silent night in two, and a shower of stars sank slowly down and went out one by one. And with a gasping sigh one word escaped the lips of the crowd: 'Rockets!' Anybody knows what rockets at sea mean. And presently another, and then a third. It is no use denying the dramatic intensity of the scene: separate it if you can from all the terrible events that followed, and picture the calmness of the night, the sudden light on the decks crowded with people in different stages of dress and undress, the background of huge funnels and tapering masts revealed by the soaring rocket, whose flash illumined at the same time the faces and minds of the obedient crowd, the one with mere physical light, the other with a sudden revelation of what its message was. Everyone knew without being told that we were calling for help from anyone who was near enough to see.

The crew were now in the boats, the sailors standing by the pulley ropes let them slip through the cleats in jerks, and down the boats went till level with B deck; women and children climbed over the rail into the boats and filled them; when full, they were lowered one by one, beginning with number 9, the first on the second class deck, and working backwards towards 15. All this we could see by peering over the edge of the boat deck, which was now quite open to the sea, the four boats which formed a natural barrier being lowered from the deck and leaving it exposed.

About this time, while walking the deck, I saw two ladies come over from the port side and walk towards the rail separating the second class from the first class deck. There stood an officer barring the way. 'May we pass to the boats?' they said. 'No, madam,' he replied politely, 'your boats are down on your own deck,' pointing to where they swung below. The ladies turned and went towards the stairway, and no doubt were able to enter one of the boats: they had ample time. I mention this to show that there was, at any rate, some arrangement – whether official or not – for separating the classes in embarking in boats; how far it was carried out, I do not know, but if the second class ladies were not expected to enter a boat from the first class deck, while steerage passengers were allowed access to the second class deck, it would seem to press rather hardly on the second class men, and this is rather supported by the low percentage saved. [While steerage passengers did find their way to other decks than their own, there is good evidence that some means were adopted to prevent them wandering at will to every part of the ship. An officer was stationed at the head of the stairs leading from the steerage deck to prevent steerage passengers climbing up to decks above – perhaps to lessen the possibility of a rush for the boats. Presently the boat to which he was assigned was being filled, and seeing it ready to go down, he said, 'There goes my boat! But I can't be in two places at the same time, and I have to keep this crowd back.']

Almost immediately after this incident, a report went round among men on the top deck – the starboard side – that men were to be taken off on the port side; how it originated, I am quite unable to say, but can only suppose that as the port boats, numbers 10 to 16, were not lowered from the top deck quite so soon as the starboard boats (they could still be seen on deck), it might be assumed that women were being taken off on one side and men on the other; but in whatever way the report started, it was acted on at once by almost all the men, who crowded across to the port side and watched the preparation for lowering the boats, leaving the starboard side almost deserted. Two or three men remained, however: not for any reason that we were consciously aware of; I can personally think of no decision arising from reasoned thought that induced me to remain rather than to cross over. But while there was no process of conscious reason at work, I am convinced that what was my salvation was a recognition of the necessity of being quiet and waiting in patience for some opportunity of safety to present itself.

Soon after the men had left the starboard side, I saw a bandsman – the cellist – come round the vestibule corner from the staircase entrance and run down the now deserted starboard deck, his cello trailing behind him, the spike dragging along the floor. This must have been about 12.40 a.m. I suppose the band must have begun to play soon after this and gone on until after 2 a.m. Many brave things were done that night, but none more brave than by those few men playing minute after minute as the ship settled quietly lower and lower in the sea and the sea rose higher and higher to where they stood; the music they played serving alike as their own immortal requiem and their right to be recorded on the rolls of undying fame.

Looking forward and downward, we could see several of the boats now in the water, moving slowly one by one from the side, without confusion or noise, and stealing away in the darkness which swallowed them in turn as the crew bent to the oars. An officer – I think First Officer Murdock – came striding along the deck, clad in a long coat, from his manner and face evidently in great agitation, but determined and resolute; he looked over the side and shouted to the boats being lowered: 'Lower away, and when afloat, row around to the gangway and wait for orders.' 'Aye, aye, sir,' was the reply; and the officer passed by and went across the ship to the port side.

Almost immediately after this, I heard a cry from below of, 'Any more ladies?' and looking over the edge of the deck, saw boat 13 swinging level with the rail of B deck, with the crew, some stokers, a few men passengers and the rest ladies – the latter being about half the total number; the boat was almost full and just about to be lowered. The call for ladies was repeated twice again, but apparently there were none to be found. Just then one of the crew looked up and saw me looking over. 'Any ladies on your deck?' he said. 'No,' I replied. 'Then you had better jump.' I sat on the edge of the deck with my feet over, threw the dressing gown (which I had carried on my arm all of the time) into the boat, dropped, and fell in the boat near the stern.

As I picked myself up, I heard a shout: 'Wait a moment, here are two more ladies,' and they were pushed hurriedly over the side and tumbled into the boat, one into the middle and one next to me in the stern. They told me afterwards that they had been assembled on a lower deck with other ladies, and had come up to B deck not by the usual stairway inside, but by one of the vertically upright iron ladders that connect each deck with the one below it, meant for the use of sailors passing about the ship. Other ladies had been in front of them and got up quickly, but these two were delayed a long time by the fact that one of them – the one that was helped first over the side into boat 13 near the middle – was not at all active: it seemed almost impossible for her to climb up a vertical ladder. We saw her trying to climb the swinging rope ladder up the *Carpathia*'s side a few hours later, and she had the same difficulty.

As they tumbled in, the crew shouted, 'Lower away'; but before the order was obeyed, a man with his wife and a baby came quickly to the side: the baby was handed to the lady in the stern, the mother got in near the middle and the father at the last moment dropped in as the boat began its journey down to the sea many feet below.

4

The Sinking of the *Titanic*, Seen From a Lifeboat

Looking back now on the descent of our boat down the ship's side, it is a matter of surprise, I think, to all the occupants to remember how little they thought of it at the time. It was a great adventure, certainly: it was exciting to feel the boat sink by jerks, foot by foot, as the ropes were paid out from above and shrieked as they passed through the pulley blocks, the new ropes and gear creaking under the strain of a boat laden with people, and the crew calling to the sailors above as the boat tilted slightly, now at one end, now at the other, 'Lower aft!' 'Lower stern!' and 'Lower together!' as she came level again – but I do not think we felt much apprehension about reaching the water safely. It certainly was thrilling to see the black hull of the ship on one side and the sea, seventy feet below, on the other, or to pass down by cabins and saloons brilliantly lighted; but we knew nothing of the apprehension felt in the minds of some of the officers whether the boats and lowering-gear would stand the strain of the weight of our sixty people. The ropes, however, were new and strong, and the boat did not buckle in the middle as an older boat might have done. Whether it was right or not to lower boats full of people to the water, – and it seems likely it was not, – I think there can be nothing but the highest praise given to the officers and crew above for the way in which they lowered the boats one after the other safely to the water; it may seem a simple matter, to read about such a thing, but any sailor knows, apparently, that it is not so. An experienced officer has told me that he has seen a boat lowered in practice from a ship's deck, with a trained crew and no passengers in the boat, with practised sailors paying out the ropes, in daylight, in calm weather, with the ship lying in dock – and has seen the boat tilt over and pitch the crew headlong into the sea. Contrast these conditions with those obtaining that Monday morning at 12.45 a.m., and it is impossible not to feel that, whether the lowering crew were trained or not, whether they had or had not drilled since coming on board, they did their duty in a way that argues the greatest efficiency. I cannot help feeling the deepest gratitude to the two sailors who stood at the ropes above and lowered us to the sea: I do not suppose they were saved.

Perhaps one explanation of our feeling little sense of the unusual in leaving the *Titanic* in this way was that it seemed the climax to a series of extraordinary occurrences: the magnitude of the whole thing dwarfed events that in the ordinary way would seem to be full of imminent peril. It is easy to imagine it – a voyage of four days on a calm sea, without a single untoward incident; the presumption, perhaps already mentally half realised, that we should be ashore in forty-eight hours and so complete a splendid voyage – and then to feel the engine stop, to be summoned on deck with little time to dress, to tie on a lifebelt, to see rockets shooting aloft in call for help, to be told to get into a lifeboat – after all these things, it did not seem much to feel the boat sinking down to the sea: it was the natural sequence of previous events, and we had learned in the last hour to take things just as they came. At the same time, if anyone should wonder what the sensation is like, it is quite easy to measure seventy-five feet from the windows of a tall house or a block of flats, look down to the ground and fancy himself with some sixty other people crowded into a boat so tightly that he could not sit down or move about, and then picture the boat sinking down in a continuous series of jerks, as the sailors pay out the ropes through cleats above. There are more pleasant sensations than this! How thankful we were that the sea was calm and the *Titanic* lay so steadily and quietly as we dropped down her side. We were spared the bumping and grinding against the side which so often accompanies the launching of boats: I do not remember that we even had to fend off our boat while we were trying to get free.

As we went down, one of the crew shouted, 'We are just over the condenser exhaust: we don't want to stay in that long or we shall be swamped; feel down on the floor and be ready to pull up the pin which lets the ropes free as soon as we are afloat.' I had often looked over the side and noticed this stream of water coming out of the side of the *Titanic* just above the waterline: in fact so large was the volume of water that as we ploughed along and met the waves coming towards us, this stream would cause a splash that sent spray flying. We felt, as well as we could in the crowd of people, on the floor, along the sides, with no idea where the pin could be found – and none of the crew knew where it was, only of its existence somewhere – but we never found it. And all the time we got closer to the sea and the exhaust roared nearer and nearer – until finally we floated with the ropes still holding us from above, the exhaust washing us away and the force of the tide driving us back against the side – the latter not of much account in influencing the direction, however. Thinking over what followed, I imagine we must have touched the water with the condenser stream at our bows, and not in the middle as I thought at one time: at any rate, the resultant of these three forces was that we were carried parallel to the ship, directly under the place where boat 15 would drop from her davits into the sea. Looking up we saw her already coming down rapidly from B deck: she must have filled almost immediately after ours. We shouted up, 'Stop lowering 15,' (In an account which appeared in the newspapers of 19 April I have described this boat as 14, not knowing they were numbered alternately.) and the crew and passengers in the boat above, hearing us shout and seeing our position immediately below them, shouted the same to the sailors on the boat deck; but apparently they did not hear, for she dropped down foot by foot – twenty feet, fifteen, ten, – and a stoker and I in the bows reached up and touched her bottom swinging above our heads, trying to push away our boat from under her. It seemed now as if nothing could prevent her dropping on us, but at this moment another stoker sprang with his knife to the ropes that still held us and I heard him shout, 'One! Two!' as he cut them through. The next moment we had swung away from underneath 15, and were clear of her as she dropped into the water in the space we had just before occupied. I do not know how the bow ropes were freed, but imagine that they were cut in the same way, for we were washed clear of the *Titanic* at once by the force of the stream and floated away as the oars were got out.

I think we all felt that that was quite the most exciting thing we had yet been through, and a great sigh of relief and gratitude went up as we swung away from the boat above our heads; but I heard no one cry aloud during the experience – not a woman's voice was raised in fear or hysteria. I think we all learnt many things that night about the bogey called 'fear', and how the facing of it is much less than the dread of it.

The crew was made up of cooks and stewards, mostly the former, I think; their white jackets showing up in the darkness as they pulled away, two to an oar: I do not think they can have had any practice in rowing, for all night long their oars crossed and clashed; if our safety had depended on speed or accuracy in keeping time it would have gone hard with us. Shouting began from one end of the boat to the other as to what we should do, where we should go, and no one seemed to have any knowledge how to act. At last we asked, 'Who is in charge of this boat?' but there was no reply. We then agreed by general consent that the stoker who stood in the stern with the tiller should act as captain, and from that time he directed the course, shouting to other boats and keeping in touch with them. Not that there was anywhere to go or anything we could do. Our plan of action was simple: to keep all the boats together as far as possible and wait until we were picked up by other liners. The crew had apparently heard of the wireless communications before they left the *Titanic*, but I never heard them say that we were in touch with any boat but the *Olympic*: it was always the *Olympic* that was coming to our rescue. They thought they knew even her distance, and making a calculation, we came to the conclusion that we ought to be picked up by her about two o'clock in the afternoon. But this was not our only hope of rescue: we watched all the time the darkness lasted for steamers' lights, thinking there might be a chance of other steamers coming near enough to see the lights which some of our boats carried. I am sure there was no feeling in the minds of anyone that we should not be picked up next day: we knew that wireless messages would go out from ship to ship, and as one of the stokers said: 'The sea will be covered with ships tomorrow afternoon: they will race up from all over the sea to find us.' Some even thought that fast torpedo boats might run up ahead of the *Olympic*. And yet the *Olympic* was, after all, the farthest away of them all; eight other ships lay within three hundred miles of us.

How thankful we should have been to know how near help was, and how many ships had heard our message and were rushing to the *Titanic*'s aid. I think nothing has surprised us more than to learn so many ships were near enough to rescue us in a few hours.

Almost immediately after leaving the *Titanic* we saw what we all said was a ship's lights down on the horizon on the *Titanic*'s port side: two lights, one above the other, and plainly not one of our boats; we even rowed in that direction for some time, but the lights drew away and disappeared below the horizon.

But this is rather anticipating: we did none of these things first. We had no eyes for anything but the ship we had just left. As the oarsmen pulled slowly away we all turned and took a long look at the mighty vessel towering high above our midget boat, and I know it must have been the most extraordinary sight I shall ever be called upon to witness; I realise now how totally inadequate language is to convey to some other person who was not there any real impression of what we saw.

But the task must be attempted: the whole picture is so intensely dramatic that, while it is not possible to place on paper for eyes to see the actual likeness of the ship as she lay there, some sketch of the scene will be possible. First of all, the climatic conditions were extraordinary. The night was one of the most beautiful I have ever seen: the sky without a single cloud to mar the perfect brilliance of the stars, clustered so thickly together that in places there seemed almost more dazzling points of light set in the black sky than background of sky itself; and each star seemed, in the keen atmosphere, free from any haze, to have increased its brilliance tenfold and to twinkle and glitter with a staccato flash that made the sky seem nothing but a setting made for them in which to display their wonder. They seemed so near, and their light so much more intense than ever before, that fancy suggested they saw this beautiful ship in dire distress below and all their energies had awakened to flash messages across the black dome of the sky to each other; telling and warning of the calamity happening in the world beneath. Later, when the *Titanic* had gone down and we lay still on the sea waiting for the day to dawn or a ship to come, I remember looking up at the perfect sky and realising why Shakespeare wrote the beautiful words he puts in the mouth of Lorenzo:

> Jessica, look how the floor of heaven
> Is thick inlaid with patines of bright gold.
> There's not the smallest orb which thou behold'st
> But in his motion like an angel sings,
> Still quiring to the young-eyed cherubims;
> Such harmony is in immortal souls;
> But whilst this muddy vesture of decay
> Doth grossly close it in, we cannot hear it.

But it seemed almost as if we could – that night: the stars seemed really to be alive and to talk. The complete absence of haze produced a phenomenon I had never seen before: where the sky met the sea the line was as clear and definite as the edge of a knife, so that the water and the air never merged gradually into each other and blended to a softened rounded horizon, but each element was so exclusively separate that where a star came low down in the sky near the clear-cut edge of the waterline, it still lost none of its brilliance. As the earth revolved and the water edge came up and covered partially the star, as it were, it simply cut the star in two, the upper half continuing to sparkle as long as it was not entirely hidden, and throwing a long beam of light along the sea to us.

In the evidence before the United States Senate Committee the captain of one of the ships near us that night said the stars were so extraordinarily bright near the horizon that he was deceived into thinking that they were ships' lights: he did not remember seeing such a night before. Those who were afloat will all agree with that statement: *we* were often deceived into thinking they were lights of a ship.

And next the cold air! Here again was something quite new to us: there was not a breath of wind to blow keenly round us as we stood in the boat, and because of its continued persistence to make us feel cold; it was just a keen, bitter, icy, motionless cold that came from nowhere and yet was there all the time; the stillness of it – if one can imagine 'cold' being motionless and still – was what seemed new and strange.

And these – the sky and the air – were overhead; and below was the sea. Here again something uncommon: the surface was like a lake of oil, heaving gently up and down with a quiet motion that rocked our boat dreamily to and fro. We did not need to keep her head to the swell: often I watched her lying broadside on to the tide, and with a boat loaded as we were, this would have been impossible with anything like a swell. The sea slipped away smoothly under the boat, and I think we never heard it lapping on the sides, so oily in appearance was the water. So when one of the stokers said he had been to sea for twenty-six years and never yet seen such a calm night, we accepted it as true without comment. Just as expressive was the remark of another – 'It reminds me of a bloomin' picnic!' It was quite true; it did: a picnic on a lake, or a quiet inland river like the Cam, or a backwater on the Thames.

And so in these conditions of sky and air and sea, we gazed broadside on the *Titanic* from a short distance. She was absolutely still – indeed from the first it seemed as if the blow from the iceberg had taken all the courage out of her and she had just come quietly to rest and was settling

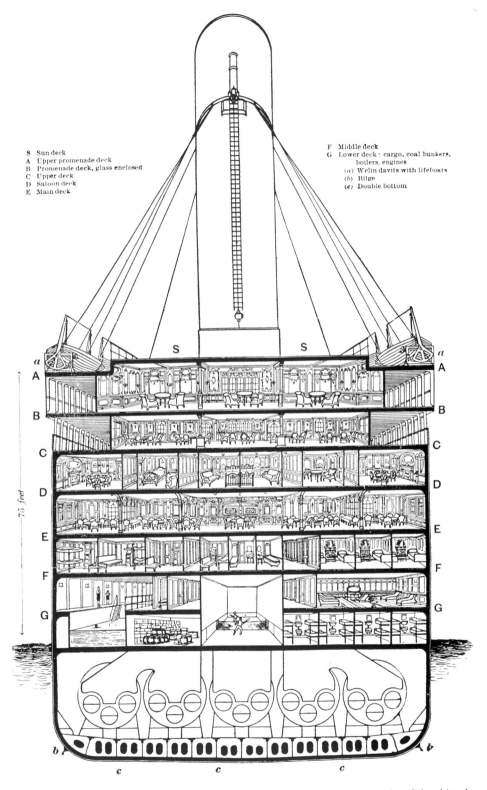

S Sun deck
A Upper promenade deck
B Promenade deck, glass enclosed
C Upper deck
D Saloon deck
E Main deck

F Middle deck
G Lower deck: cargo, coal bunkers,
  boilers, engines
  (a) Welin davits with lifeboats
  (b) Bilge
  (c) Double bottom

1. Transverse amidship section through the *Titanic* showing the various decks of the ship, the indoor squash court, swimming pool and third class living quarters. This was reproduced in the 1912 edition of Lawrence's book.

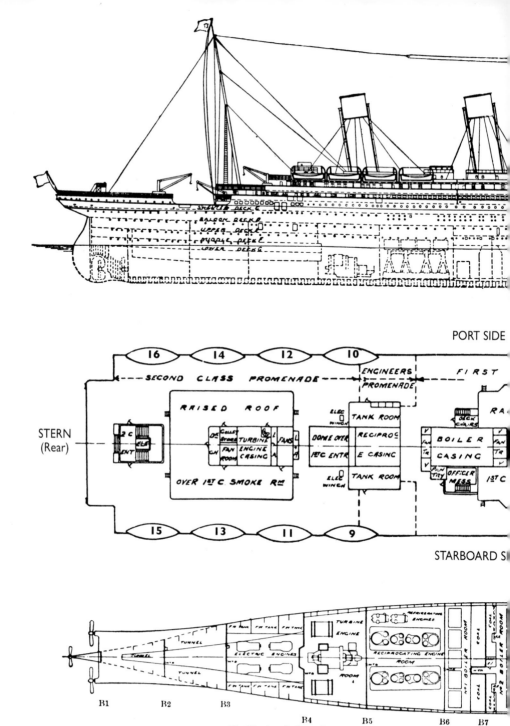

PORT SIDE

STERN
(Rear)

16 14 12 10

SECOND CLASS PROMENADE

ENGINEERS
PROMENADE

FIRST

RRISED ROOF

ELEC
WINCH

TANK ROOM

DECK
CHAIRS

RA

2C
ENT

ELS
CN

GALLEY
STORE
FAN ENGINE
ROOM

TURBINE
ENGINE
CASING

FANS

OVER 1ST C. SMOKE RM

DOME OVER
REC ENTR

ELEC
WINCH

RECIPROS
E CASING

TANK ROOM

V
TR

V
TR

BOILER

CASING

FAN

FAN

FAN
TR

OFFICER
MESS

1ST C

15 13 11 9

STARBOARD S

B1   B2   B3   B4   B5   B6   B7

TURBINE
ENGINE

REFRIGERATING
ENGINES

FW TANK FW TANK FW TANK

TUNNEL

ELECTRIC ENGINES
ROOM

RECIPROCATING ENGINE
ROOM

NO1 BOILER
ROOM

COAL

TUNNEL

TUNNEL

FW TANK FW TANK

ROOM

COAL

COAL

NO2 BOILER

COAL

Top page spread: 2. Longitudinal section of the *Titanic* from the Harland & Wolff blueprints c. 1911. Bridge deck B through to lower deck G are marked.

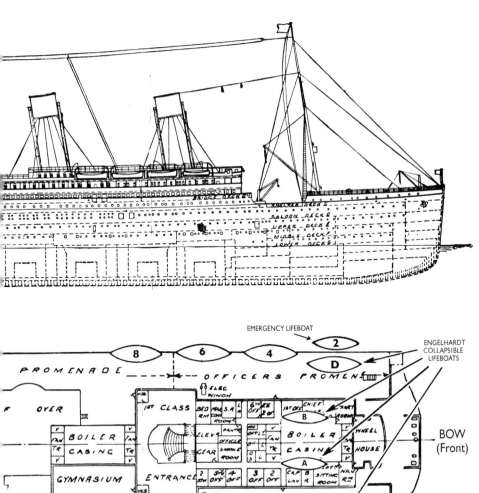

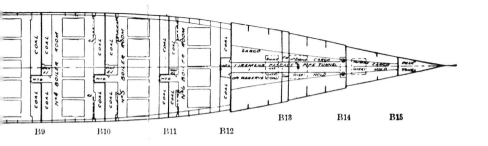

Middle page spread: 3. Plan of the boat deck of the *Titanic* showing the position of all 20 lifeboats, 1 to 16 and collapsibles A, B, C & D.

Above: 4. Plan of the Tank Top of the *Titanic* showing the 15 transverse bulkheads of the ship's hull which created 16 compartments, each of which could be isolated from the adjoining compartment by a watertight door.

5. *Titanic* passing through Belfast Lough en route to the Irish Sea for her trials, 2 April 1912.

Bottom page spread: 6. *Titanic*'s near miss with the SS *New York* shortly after departing from Southampton on her maiden voyage, noon Wednesday 10 April. Lawrence was out on deck to witness the incident: 'It gave an extraordinary impression of the absolute helplessness of a big liner in the absence of any motive power to guide her.'

Above: 7. The *Titanic* ablaze with lights heading out of Cherbourg harbour on 10 April. Lawrence Beesley: 'In the calmest weather we made Cherbourg just as it grew dusk and left again about 8.30 p.m., after taking on board passengers and mails.'

Right: 8. Captain of the *Titanic*, Edward Smith.

Left: 9. View of the forecastle. Lawrence: 'All the boats were lowered and sent away by about a.m. and by this time the ship wa very low in the water, the forecas deck completely submerged, and the sea creeping steadily up to the bridge and probably only a few yards away.'

Below: 10. *Titanic*'s near-identica sister ship, *Olympic*. This shows the layout of the forward starboa lifeboats, from left to right in this picture, 7, 5, 3, with 1 next, and C just visible behind lifeboat 1. Note the proximity to the bridge. Collapsible lifeboat A is not visib but is stowed alongside the funne

Above: 11. Promenade deck which ran nearly the whole length of the ship. Many female passengers were loaded into lifeboats from this deck.

Right: 12. Forward starboard boat deck. On Good Friday, 5 April 1912, the liner was thrown open to the public for the day in Southampton. This was the only occasion the ship was dressed overall in flags. The lifeboats shown are 3 (nearest), 5 and 7. In the distance can be seen lifeboats 9, 11, 13 (the lifeboat Lawrence escaped on) and 15. The exit onto the boat deck from the gym and grand staircase is opposite lifeboat 7.

Left: 13. After deck *Olympic* 1911. View towards decks at the stern of the ship. Helen Bishop (lifeboat 7) describes the last moments of the *Titanic*: 'When the forward part of the ship dropped suddenly at a faster rate so that the upward slope became marked there was a sudden rush of passengers on all decks toward the stern. It was like a wave. We could see great black mass of people in the steerage sweeping to the rear part of the boat... Then it began to slide gently downwards. Its speed increased as it went down head first, so that the stern shot down with a rush. We could see the people packed densely in the stern till it was gone.'

Below: 14. *Olympic*, showing the layout of the r starboard lifeboats, from left to right in this pict 15, 13 (which Lawrence left *Titanic* on), 11 and

above: 15. Rear starboard boat deck and the second class
promenade area. The lifeboats shown are 15 (nearest), 13, 11
and 9. Lawrence: 'I was now on the starboard side of the top
boat deck; the time about 12.20 a.m. We watched the crew
work on the lifeboats, numbers 9, 11, 13, 15, some inside
arranging the oars, some coiling ropes on the deck, the ropes
which ran through the pulleys to lower to the sea, others with
cranks fitted to the rocking arms of the davits. As we watched,
the cranks were turned, the davits swung outwards until the
boats hung clear of the edge of the deck. Just then an officer
came along from the first class deck and shouted above the noise
of escaping steam, "All women and children get down to deck
below and all men stand back from the boats." The men fell
back and the women retired below to get into the boats from
the next deck.'

right: 16. Four decks of *Olympic*. Note the stairs from the deck
used by steerage passengers up to the lower promenade deck.
Lawrence: 'Looking down astern from the boat deck or from
the deck to the steerage quarters, I often noticed how the third
class passengers were enjoying every minute of the time... [an]
interesting man was travelling steerage, but had placed his wife
in the second cabin: he would climb the stairs leading from the
steerage to the second deck and talk affectionately with his wife
across the low gate which separated them. I never saw him after
the collision, but I think his wife was on the *Carpathia*. Whether
they ever saw each other on the Sunday night is very doubtful:
he would not at first be allowed on the second class deck, and
if he were, the chances of seeing his wife in the darkness and
the crowd would be very small, indeed. Of all those playing
so happily on the steerage deck I did not recognise many
afterwards on the *Carpathia*.'

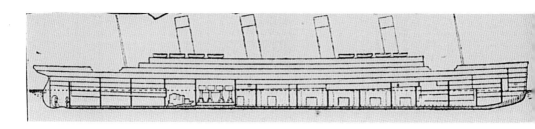

Top spread: 17. Cutaway drawing of *Titanic* reproduced in newspapers in late April 1912.

Above: 18. Contemporary drawing of *Titanic* showing her 15 transverse bulkheads.

Below: 19. *Titanic* in Belfast Harbour.

20. *Titanic* proceeding down Southampton Water on its maiden voyage, 10 April. Although *Titanic* was the most luxurious ship in the world she carried 20 lifeboats, enough for 1,178 passengers. On her maiden voyage to New York she was carrying over 2,200 people.

21. Forward first class grand stairway immortalised in the *Titanic* film. The top landing led out directly onto the boat deck. Elizabeth Shutes, lifeboat 3: 'How different are these staircases now! No laughing throng, but on either side stand quietly, bravely, the stewards, all equipped with the white, ghostly life preservers.'

22. Bedroom of the parlor suite on board *Titanic*.

23. First class dining room (or dining saloon).

24. This photograph from the *Olympic* reveals how the first class smoking room on the *Titanic* would have looked.

Opposite page: 25. An over-dramatic depiction of the *Titanic* striking the iceberg head on. From a French journal, April 1912. Lawrence complained of the inaccurate potrayal of the disaster in the newspapers of the time.

Above: 26. A contemporary illustration of *Titanic*'s hull being struck below the waterline by the underwater mass of the iceberg. A more accurate portrayal of the collision.

Below: 27. Cartoon from a 1912 newspaper about the *Titanic* disaster showing the despair of wives being physically parted from their husbands by the crew and put aboard the lifeboats. Lawrence witnessed just such a drama: 'Two women refused at first to leave their husbands, but partly by persuasion and partly by force they were separated from them and sent down to the next deck.'

28. Lawrence: 'I think there can be nothing but the highest praise given to the officers and crew above for the way in which they lowered the boats one after the other safely to the water; it may seem a simple matter, to read about such a thing, but any sailor knows, apparently, that it is not so. An experienced officer has told me that he has seen a boat lowered in practice from a ship's deck, with practiced sailors paying out the ropes, in daylight and has seen the boat tilt over and pitch the crew headlong into the sea. Contrast these conditions with those obtaining that Monday morning at 12.45 a.m., and it is impossible not to feel that, whether they had or had not drilled since coming on board, they did their duty in a way that argues the greatest efficiency. I cannot help feeling the deepest gratitude to the two sailors who stood at the ropes above and lowered us to the sea: I do not suppose they were saved.'

TENNIS COURTS ON THE
UPPER DECK
TURKISH BATHS 4TH DECK
PORT SIDE
GYMNASIUM LOWER DECK AFT
SUN PARLOR UPPER DECK AFT
BALL ROOM 3RD DECK
CONCERT SALOON AND THEATRE
5TH DECK
BILLIARD ROOM 6TH DECK AFT

—*Detroit News*

EVERYTHING FOR ENJOYING LIFE, BUT NOT MUCH TO SAVE IT

29. Cartoon from a 1912 newspaper about the *Titanic* disaster; the irony is obvious.

30. & 31. The lowering of the lifeboats. It was 75 feet from the boat deck to the sea, a distance that decreased as the night wore on and the *Titanic* sank lower and lower in the water.

32. Lawrence on the plight of passengers in the freezing Atlantic waters: 'The cries of the drowning floating across the quiet sea filled us with stupefaction: we longed to return and rescue at least some of the drowning, but we knew it was impossible. The boat was filled to standing-room, and to return would mean the swamping of us all, and so the captain-stoker told his crew to row away from the cries. We tried to sing to keep all from thinking of them; but there was no heart for singing in the boat at that time. The cries, which were loud and numerous at first, died away gradually one by one, but the night was clear, frosty and still. I think the last of them must have been heard nearly forty minutes after the *Titanic* sank. Lifebelts would keep the survivors afloat for hours; but the cold water was what stopped the cries.'

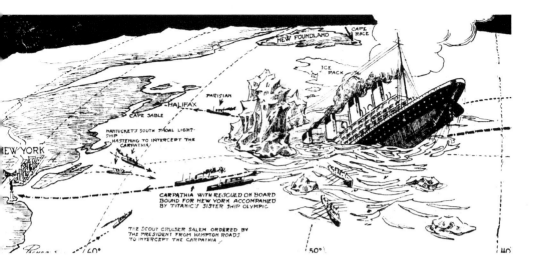

33. A contemporary newspaper depiction of the location of the sinking of the *Titanic* and positions of other ships in the area.

34. Contemporary illustration showing the *Titanic*'s two wireless operators working the Marconi set as water washes over the boat deck.

11 45 P.M.

STRIKES STARBOARD BOW -12 ⁴ⁿ AFT

SETTLES BY HEAD - BOATS ORDERED OUT 12 05 A.M

—1 40 A.M.

SETTLES TO FORWARD STACK
BREAKS BETWEEN STACKS

This page & opposite page: 35, 36, 37, 38, 39 & 40. Series of sketches executed on board *Carpathia* by Lewis Skidmore (a young art teacher), based on conversations with *Titanic* survivor Jack Thayer following the rescue. Jack Thayer was one of a number of survivors to describe the ship breaking in two as she sank. Lawrence Beesley refuted this assessment but seventy years later Thayer and others was proved right when the wreck was discovered resting on the seabed in two halves.

FORWARD END FLOATS,
THEN SINKS

1.50 A.M

STERN SECTION:
PIVETS AMIDSHIPS AND
SWINGS OVER SPOT WHERE FORWARD SECTION SANK

2.00 A.M

LAST POSITION
IN WHICH "TITANIC"
STAYED 5 MINUTES BEFORE
THE FINAL PLUNGE

R. Skidmore
S.S. "Carpathia" Apr 15th
1912.

41. *Titanic* survivors in one of the lifeboats approaching the *Carpathia*. Possibly lifeboat 6, as Quartermaster Hichens wore a blanket and was at the tiller.

42. Lifeboat 14 towing collapsible lifeboat D towards *Carpathia*.

43. *Titanic* survivors in collapsible lifeboat D, one of the last to be launched at *c.* 2.05 am.

44. *Titanic* survivors in a lifeboat.

Opposite: 45. Lawrence: 'The surface was like a lake of oil, heaving gently up and down with a quiet motion that rocked our boat dreamily to and fro. We did not need to keep her head to the swell: often I watched her lying broadside on to the tide, and with a boat loaded as we were, this would have been impossible with anything like a swell. So when one of the stokers said he had been to sea for twenty-six years and never yet seen such a calm night, we accepted it as true.'

Images on this page: 46, 47, 48 & 49. Four candidates photographed in the immediate aftermath of the sinking for 'iceberg that sank the *Titanic*'. These photographs were reproduced around the world in newspapers and books.

Images on this page: 50, 51 & 52. Views of two lifeboats alongside the *Carpathia*. One is clearly far from full, the other looks overloaded. Captain Rostron of the *Carpathia*: 'They started climbing aboard. Obviously they had got away in a hurry, for there were only twenty-five of them whereas the capacity of the boat was fully forty.' Lawrence's lifeboat reached *Carpathia* at about 4.30 a.m.

Above: 53. Photograph of the *Carpathia* with the recovered *Titanic* lifeboats aboard.

Right: 54. *Carpathia*'s deck strewn with lifeboats.

Below: 55. Group of survivors of the *Titanic* disaster aboard the *Carpathia* after being rescued. Howard Chapin, *Carpathia* passenger: 'Practically everyone was quiet and subdued, apparently stunned by the shock and the cold.'

56. Lawrence on the state of mind of survivors as they boarded *Carpathia*: 'The hysterical scenes that have been described are imaginative; true, one woman did fill the saloon with hysterical cries immediately after coming aboard, but she could not have known for a certainty that any of her friends were lost: probably the sense of relief after some hours of journeying about the sea was too much for her for a time.'

57. Harold Bride, surviving wireless operator of the *Titanic*, with feet bandaged, being carried up ramp of ship. He was washed off the deck of the *Titanic* just as it sank but managed to attach himself to the upturned hull of collapsible lifeboat B: 'There were men all around me – hundreds of them. The sea was dotted with them, all depending on their lifebelts.'

Above: 58. The Navatril children, Michel and Edmond, passengers on the *Titanic* who had been abducted by their father, here returned to their mother. Lawrence observed the two children playing in the covered corridor outside the library. They escaped the sinking ship in lifeboat D; their father perished. To board the ship, their father assumed the name Louis Hoffman and used their nicknames, Lolo and Mamon.

Above left: 59. American Colonel Archibald Gracie was one of the few passengers to have survived in the freezing waters before scrambling onto the upturned lifeboat B. he describes vividly how he went down with the ship: 'I was in a whirlpool of water, swirling round and round, as I still tried to cling to the railing as the ship plunged to the depths below. Down, down, I went.' Like Lawrence, he would go on to write his memoirs of how he survived the sinking.
Above right: 60. Another noted *Titanic* victim, first class passenger Archibald Butt, military aid to two US presidents. Lawrence states in his account that reports of Butt beating back a crowd rushing a lifeboat with a pistol were media exaggerations.

Above left: 61. Herbert Pitman, third officer of *Titanic* testifying before the US Senate investigation into the sinking. Lawrence incorrectly refers to him as the fouth officer.

Above right: 62. John Phillips, senior wireless operator on *Titanic* who perished.

Below: 63. Major Peuchen gets a mention in Lawrence's account. He is identified as [4] in this photograph of the US Senate investigation. [5] is Herbert Pitman and [6] is P. A. S. Franklin, White Star Line Vice President. When the New York office of the White Star Line was informed that *Titanic* was in trouble, he announced, 'We place absolute confidence in the *Titanic*. We believe the boat is unsinkable.' By the time Franklin spoke those words *Titanic* was at the bottom of the ocean.

64. Bruce Ismay, Managing Director of the White Star Line and fellow survivor of the sinking, being questioned by the Senate Investigating Committee.

65. The day after they had been picked up, Lawrence together with other survivors met in the saloon of *Carpathia* and established a committee to collect donations to aid survivors and crew in hardship. They also paid for the 'loving cup' presented here on 29 May 1912 by the 'unsinkable' Molly (Margaret) Brown to Captain Roston, for his service in the rescue of the *Titanic*.

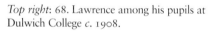

Above: 66. Lawrence Beesley as a young man.

Below: 67. Lawrence and his children on the golf course. From left to right: Hugh, Laurien (Nicholas Wade's mother), Lawrence, Dinah, Lawrence's wife Muriel and Waveney (about to swing).

Top right: 68. Lawrence among his pupils at Dulwich College *c.* 1908.

down without an effort to save herself, without a murmur of protest against such a foul blow. For the sea could not rock her: the wind was not there to howl noisily round the decks, and make the ropes hum; from the first what must have impressed all as they watched was the sense of stillness about her and the slow, insensible way she sank lower and lower in the sea, like a stricken animal.

The mere bulk alone of the ship viewed from the sea below was an awe-inspiring sight. Imagine a ship nearly a sixth of a mile long, 75 feet high to the top decks, with four enormous funnels above the decks, and masts again high above the funnels; with her hundreds of portholes, all her saloons and other rooms brilliant with light, and all round her, little boats filled with those who until a few hours before had trod her decks and read in her libraries and listened to the music of her band in happy content; and who were now looking up in amazement at the enormous mass above them and rowing away from her because she was sinking.

I had often wanted to see her from some distance away, and only a few hours before, in conversation at lunch with a fellow passenger, had registered a vow to get a proper view of her lines and dimensions when we landed at New York: to stand some distance away to take in a full view of her beautiful proportions, which the narrow approach to the dock at Southampton made impossible. Little did I think that the opportunity was to be found so quickly and so dramatically. The background, too, was a different one from what I had planned for her: the black outline of her profile against the sky was bordered all round by stars studded in the sky, and all her funnels and masts were picked out in the same way: her bulk was seen where the stars were blotted out. And one other thing was different from expectation: the thing that ripped away from us instantly, as we saw it, all sense of the beauty of the night, the beauty of the ship's lines, and the beauty of her lights – and all these taken in themselves were intensely beautiful – that thing was the awful angle made by the level of the sea with the rows of porthole lights along her side in dotted lines, row above row. The sea level and the rows of lights should have been parallel – should never have met – and now they met at an angle inside the black hull of the ship. There was nothing else to indicate she was injured; nothing but this apparent violation of a simple geometrical law – that parallel lines should 'never meet even if produced ever so far both ways'; but it meant the *Titanic* had sunk by the head until the lowest portholes in the bows were under the sea, and the portholes in the stern were lifted above the normal height. We rowed away from her in the quietness of the night, hoping and praying with all our hearts that she would sink no more and the day would find her still in the same position as she was then. The crew, however, did not think so. It has been said frequently that the officers and crew felt assured that she would remain afloat even after they knew the extent of the damage. Some of them may have done so – and perhaps, from their scientific knowledge of her construction, with more reason at the time than those who said she would sink – but at any rate the stokers in our boat had no such illusion. One of them – I think he was the same man that cut us free from the pulley ropes – told us how he was at work in the stokehole, and in anticipation of going off duty in quarter of an hour – thus confirming the time of the collision as 11.45 – had near him a pan of soup keeping hot on some part of the machinery; suddenly the whole side of the compartment came in, and the water rushed him off his feet. Picking himself up, he sprang for the compartment doorway and was just through the aperture when the watertight door came down behind him, 'like a knife,' as he said; 'they work them from the bridge.' He had gone up on deck but was ordered down again at once and with others was told to draw the fires from under the boiler, which they did, and were then at liberty to come on deck again. It seems that this particular knot of stokers must have known almost as soon as anyone of the extent of injury. He added mournfully, 'I could do with that hot soup now' – and indeed he could: he was clad at the time of the collision, he said, in trousers and singlet, both very thin on account of the intense heat in the stokehole; and although he had added a short jacket later, his teeth were chattering with the cold. He found a place to lie down underneath the tiller on the little platform where our captain stood, and there he lay all night with a coat belonging to another stoker thrown over him and I think he must have been almost unconscious. A lady next to him, who was warmly clad with several coats, tried to insist on his having one of hers – a fur-lined one – thrown over him, but he absolutely refused while some of the women were insufficiently clad; and so the coat was given to an Irish girl with pretty auburn hair standing near, leaning against the gunwale – with an 'outside berth' and so more exposed to the cold air. This same lady was able to distribute more of her wraps to the passengers, a rug to one, a fur boa to another; and she has related with amusement that at the moment of climbing up the *Carpathia*'s side, those to whom these articles had been lent offered them all back to her; but as, like the rest of us, she was encumbered with a lifebelt, she had to say she would receive them back at the end of the climb, I had not seen my dressing gown since I dropped into the boat, but some time in the night a steerage passenger found it on the floor and put it on.

It is not easy at this time to call to mind who were in the boat, because in the night it was not possible to see more than a few feet away, and when dawn came we had eyes only for the rescue ship and the icebergs; but so far as my memory serves the list was as follows:

no first class passengers; three women, one baby, two men from the second cabin; and the other passengers steerage – mostly women; a total of about 35 passengers. The rest, about 25 (and possibly more), were crew and stokers. Near to me all night was a group of three Swedish girls, warmly clad, standing close together to keep warm, and very silent; indeed there was very little talking at any time.

One conversation took place that is, I think, worth repeating: one more proof that the world after all is a small place. The ten months' old baby which was handed down at the last moment was received by a lady next to me – the same who shared her wraps and coats. The mother had found a place in the middle and was too tightly packed to come through to the child, and so it slept contentedly for about an hour in a stranger's arms; it then began to cry and the temporary nurse said: 'Will you feel down and see if the baby's feet are out of the blanket! I don't know much about babies but I think their feet must be kept warm.' Wriggling down as well as I could, I found its toes exposed to the air and wrapped them well up, when it ceased crying at once: it was evidently a successful diagnosis! Having recognised the lady by her voice – it was much too dark to see faces – as one of my vis-à-vis at the purser's table, I said 'Surely you are Miss — ?' 'Yes,' she replied, 'and you must be Mr Beesley; how curious we should find ourselves in the same boat!' Remembering that she had joined the boat at Queenstown, I said, 'Do you know Clonmel? A letter from a great friend of mine who is staying there at — [giving the address] came aboard at Queenstown.' 'Yes, it is my home: and I was dining at — just before I came away.' It seemed that she knew my friend, too; and we agreed that of all places in the world to recognise mutual friends, a crowded lifeboat afloat in mid-ocean at 2 a.m. twelve hundred miles from our destination was one of the most unexpected.

And all the time, as we watched, the *Titanic* sank lower and lower by the head and the angle became wider and wider as the stern porthole lights lifted and the bow lights sank, and it was evident she was not to stay afloat much longer. The captain-stoker now told the oarsmen to row away as hard as they could. Two reasons seemed to make this a wise decision: one that as she sank she would create such a wave of suction that boats, if not sucked under by being too near, would be in danger of being swamped by the wave her sinking would create – and we all knew our boat was in no condition to ride big waves, crowded as it was and manned with untrained oarsmen. The second was that an explosion might result from the water getting to the boilers, and debris might fall within a wide radius. And yet, as it turned out, neither of these things happened.

At about 2.15 a.m. I think we were any distance from a mile to two miles away. It is difficult for a landsman to calculate distance at sea but we had been afloat an hour and a half, the boat was heavily loaded, the oarsmen unskilled, and our course erratic: following now one light and now another, sometimes a star and sometimes a light from a port lifeboat which had turned away from the *Titanic* in the opposite direction and lay almost on our horizon; and so we could not have gone very far away.

About this time, the water had crept up almost to her sidelight and the captain's bridge, and it seemed a question only of minutes before she sank. The oarsmen lay on their oars, and all in the lifeboat were motionless as we watched her in absolute silence – save some who would not look and buried their heads on each others' shoulders. The lights still shone with the same brilliance, but not so many of them: many were now below the surface. I have often wondered since whether they continued to light up the cabins when the portholes were under water; they may have done so.

And then, as we gazed awestruck, she tilted slowly up, revolving apparently about a centre of gravity just astern of amidships, until she attained a vertically upright position; and there she remained – motionless! As she swung up, her lights, which had shone without a flicker all night, went out suddenly, came on again for a single flash, then went out altogether. And as they did so, there came a noise which many people, wrongly I think, have described as an explosion; it has always seemed to me that it was nothing but the engines and machinery coming loose from their bolts and bearings, and falling through the compartments, smashing everything in their way. It was partly a roar, partly a groan, partly a rattle, and partly a smash, and it was not a sudden roar as an explosion would be: it went on successively for some seconds, possibly fifteen to twenty, as the heavy machinery dropped down to the bottom (now the bows) of the ship: I suppose it fell through the end and sank first, before the ship. But it was a noise no one had heard before, and no one wishes to hear again: it was stupefying, stupendous, as it came to us along the water. It was as if all the heavy things one could think of had been thrown downstairs from the top of a house, smashing each other and the stairs and everything in the way.

Several apparently authentic accounts have been given, in which definite stories of explosions have been related – in some cases even with wreckage blown up and the ship broken in two; but I think such accounts will not stand close analysis. In the first place the fires had been withdrawn and the steam allowed to escape some time before she sank, and the possibility of explosion from this cause seems very remote. Then, as just related, the noise was not sudden and definite, but prolonged – more like the roll and crash of thunder. The probability of the noise being caused by engines falling down will be seen by referring to illustration 4, where the engines are placed in compartments 3, 4, and 5. As the *Titanic* tilted up they would almost certainly fall loose from their bed and plunge down through the other compartments.

No phenomenon like that pictured in some American and English papers occurred – that of the ship breaking in two, and the two ends being raised above the surface. I saw these drawings in preparation on board the *Carpathia*, and said at the time that they bore no resemblance to what actually happened.

When the noise was over the *Titanic* was still upright like a column: we could see her now only as the stern and some 150 feet of her stood outlined against the star-specked sky, looming black in the darkness, and in this position she continued for some minutes – I think as much as five minutes, but it may have been less. Then, first sinking back a little at the stern, I thought, she slid slowly forwards through the water and dived slantingly down; the sea closed over her and we had seen the last of the beautiful ship on which we had embarked four days before at Southampton.

And in place of the ship on which all our interest had been concentrated for so long and towards which we looked most of the time because it was still the only object on the sea which was a fixed point to us – in place of the *Titanic*, we had the level sea now stretching in an unbroken expanse to the horizon: heaving gently just as before, with no indication on the surface that the waves had just closed over the most wonderful vessel ever built by man's hand; the stars looked down just the same and the air was just as bitterly cold.

There seemed a great sense of loneliness when we were left on the sea in a small boat without the *Titanic*: not that we were uncomfortable (except for the cold) nor in danger: we did not think we were either, but the *Titanic* was no longer there.

We waited head on for the wave which we thought might come – the wave we had heard so much of from the crew and which they said had been known to travel for miles – and it never came. But although the *Titanic* left us no such legacy of a wave as she went to the bottom, she left us something we would willingly forget forever, something which it is well not to let the imagination dwell on – the cries of many hundreds of our fellow passengers struggling in the ice-cold water.

I would willingly omit any further mention of this part of the disaster from this book, but for two reasons it is not possible – first, that as a matter of history it should be put on record; and secondly, that these cries were not only an appeal for help in the awful conditions of danger in which the drowning found themselves – an appeal that could never be answered – but an appeal to the whole world to make such conditions of danger and hopelessness impossible ever again; a cry that called to the heavens for the very injustice of its own existence; a cry that clamoured for its own destruction.

We were utterly surprised to hear this cry go up as the waves closed over the *Titanic*: we had heard no sound of any kind from her since we left her side; and, as mentioned before, we did not know how many boats she had or how many rafts. The crew may have known, but they probably did not, and if they did, they never told the passengers; we should not have been surprised to know all were safe on some lifesaving device.

So that unprepared as we were for such a thing, the cries of the drowning floating across the quiet sea filled us with stupefaction: we longed to return and rescue at least some of the drowning, but we knew it was impossible. The boat was filled to standing room, and to return would mean the swamping of us all, and so the captain-stoker told his crew to row away from the cries. We tried to sing to keep all from thinking of them; but there was no heart for singing in the boat at that time.

The cries, which were loud and numerous at first, died away gradually one by one, but the night was clear, frosty and still, the water smooth, and the sounds must have carried on its level surface free from any obstruction for miles, certainly much farther from the ship than we were situated. I think the last of them must have been heard nearly forty minutes after the *Titanic* sank. Lifebelts would keep the survivors afloat for hours; but the cold water was what stopped the cries.

There must have come to all those safe in the lifeboats, scattered round the drowning at various distances, a deep resolve that, if anything could be done by them in the future to prevent the repetition of such sounds, they would do it – at whatever cost of time or other things. And not only to them are those cries an imperative call, but to every man and woman who has known of them. It is not possible that ever again can such conditions exist; but it is a duty imperative on one and all to see that they do not. Think of it! A few more boats, a few more planks of wood nailed together in a particular way at a trifling cost, and all those men and women whom the world can so ill afford to lose would be with us today, there would be no mourning in thousands of homes which now are desolate, and these words need not have been written.

5

The Rescue

All accounts agree that the *Titanic* sank about 2.20 a.m.: a watch in our boat gave the time as 2.30 a.m. shortly afterwards. We were then in touch with three other boats: one was 15, on our starboard quarter, and the others I have always supposed were 9 and 11, but I do not know definitely. We never got into close touch with each other, but called occasionally across the darkness and saw them looming near and then drawing away again; we called to ask if any officer were aboard the other three, but did not find one. So in the absence of any plan of action, we rowed slowly forward – or what we thought was forward, for it was in the direction the *Titanic*'s bows were pointing before she sank. I see now that we must have been pointing north-west, for we presently saw the Northern Lights on the starboard, and again, when the *Carpathia* came up from the south, we saw her from behind us on the south-east, and turned our boat around to get to her. I imagine the boats must have spread themselves over the ocean fanwise as they escaped from the *Titanic*: those on the starboard and port sides forward being almost dead ahead of her and the stern boats being broadside from her; this explains why the port boats were so much longer in reaching the *Carpathia* – as late as 8.30 a.m. – while some of the starboard boats came up as early as 4.10 a.m. Some of the port boats had to row across the place where the *Titanic* sank to get to the *Carpathia*, through the debris of chairs and wreckage of all kinds.

None of the other three boats near us had a light – and we missed lights badly: we could not see each other in the darkness; we could not signal to ships which might be rushing up full speed from any quarter to the *Titanic*'s rescue; and now we had been through so much it would seem hard to have to encounter the additional danger of being in the line of a rescuing ship. We felt again for the lantern beneath our feet, along the sides, and I managed this time to get down to the locker below the tiller platform and open it in front by removing a board, to find nothing but the zinc airtank which renders the boat unsinkable when upset. I do not think there was a light in the boat. We felt also for food and water, and found none, and came to the conclusion that none had been put in; but here we were mistaken. I have a letter from Second Officer Lightoller in which he assures me that he and Fourth Officer Pitman examined every lifeboat from the *Titanic* as they lay on the *Carpathia*'s deck afterwards and found biscuits and water in each. Not that we wanted any food or water then: we thought of the time that might elapse before the *Olympic* picked us up in the afternoon.

Towards 3 a.m. we saw a faint glow in the sky ahead on the starboard quarter, the first gleams, we thought, of the coming dawn. We were not certain of the time and were eager perhaps to accept too readily any relief from darkness – only too glad to be able to look each other in the face and see who were our companions in good fortune; to be free from the hazard of lying in a steamer's track, invisible in the darkness. But we were doomed to disappointment: the soft light increased for a time, and died away a little; glowed again, and then remained stationary for some minutes! 'The Northern Lights'! It suddenly came to me, and so it was: presently the light arched fanwise across the northern sky, with faint streamers reaching towards the Polestar. I had seen them of about the same intensity in England some years ago and knew them again. A sigh of disappointment went through the boat as we realised that the day was not yet; but had we known it, something more comforting even than the day was in store for us. All night long we had watched the horizon with eager eyes for signs of a steamer's lights; we heard from the captain-stoker that the first appearance would be a single light on the horizon, the masthead light, followed shortly by a second one, lower down, on the deck; if these two remained in vertical alignment and the distance between them increased as the lights drew nearer, we might be certain it was a steamer. But what a night to see that first light on the horizon! We saw it many times as the earth revolved, and some stars rose on the clear horizon and others sank down to it: there were 'lights' on every quarter. Some we watched and followed until we saw the deception and grew wiser; some were lights from those of our boats that were fortunate enough to have lanterns, but these were generally easily detected, as they rose and fell in the near distance. Once they raised our hopes, only to sink them to zero again. Near what seemed to be the horizon on the port quarter we saw two lights close together, and thought this must be our double light; but as we gazed across the miles that separated us, the lights slowly drew apart and we realised that they were two boats' lanterns at different distances from us, in line, one behind the other. They were probably the forward port boats that had to return so many miles next morning across the *Titanic*'s graveyard.

But notwithstanding these hopes and disappointments, the absence of lights, food and water (as we thought), and the bitter cold, it would not be correct to say we were unhappy in those early morning hours: the cold that settled down on us like a garment that wraps close around was the only real discomfort, and that we could keep at bay by not thinking too much about it as well as by vigorous friction and gentle stamping on the floor (it made too much noise to stamp hard!). I never heard that anyone in boat 13 had any after effects from the cold – even the stoker who was so thinly clad came through without harm. After all, there were many things to be thankful for: so many that they made insignificant the temporary inconvenience of the cold, the crowded boat, the darkness and the hundred and one things that in the ordinary way we might regard as unpleasant. The quiet sea, the beautiful night (how different from two nights later when flashes of lightning and peals of thunder broke the sleep of many on board the *Carpathia*!), and above all the fact of being in a boat at all when so many of our fellow passengers and crew – whose cries no longer moaned across the water to us – were silent in the water. Gratitude was the dominant note in our feelings then. But grateful as we were, our gratitude was soon to be increased a hundred fold. About 3.30 a.m., as nearly as I can judge, some one in the bow called our attention to a faint faraway gleam in the south-east. We all turned quickly to look and there it was certainly: streaming up from behind the horizon like a distant flash of a warship's searchlight; then a faint boom like guns afar off, and the light died away again. The stoker who had lain all night under the tiller sat up suddenly as if from a dream, the overcoat hanging from his shoulders. I can see him now, staring out across the sea, to where the sound had come from, and hear him shout, 'That was a cannon!' But it was not: it was the *Carpathia*'s rocket, though we did not know it until later. But we did know now that something was not far away, racing up to our help and signalling to us a preliminary message to cheer our hearts until she arrived.

With every sense alert, eyes gazing intently at the horizon and ears open for the least sound, we waited in absolute silence in the quiet night. And then, creeping over the edge of the sea where the flash had been, we saw a single light, and presently a second below it, and in a few minutes they were well above the horizon and they remained in line! But we had been deceived before, and we waited a little longer before we allowed ourselves to say we were safe. The lights came up rapidly: so rapidly it seemed only a few minutes (though it must have been longer) between first seeing them and finding them well above the horizon and bearing down rapidly on us. We did not know what sort of a vessel was coming, but we knew she was coming quickly, and we searched for paper, rags – anything that would burn (we were quite prepared to burn our coats if necessary). A hasty paper torch was twisted out of letters found in someone's pocket, lighted, and held aloft by the stoker standing on the tiller platform. The little light shone in flickers on the faces of the occupants of the boat, ran in broken lines for a few yards along the black oily sea (where for the first time I saw the presence of that awful thing which had caused the whole terrible disaster – ice – in little chunks the size of one's fist, bobbing harmlessly up and down), and spluttered away to blackness again as the stoker threw the burning remnants of paper overboard. But had we known it, the danger of being run down was already over, one reason being that the *Carpathia* had already seen the lifeboat which all night long had shown a green light, the first indication the *Carpathia* had of our position. But the real reason is to be found in the *Carpathia*'s log: 'Went full speed ahead during the night; stopped at 4 a.m. with an iceberg dead ahead.' It was a good reason.

With our torch burnt and in darkness again we saw the headlights stop, and realised that the rescuer had hove to. A sigh of relief went up when we thought no hurried scramble had to be made to get out of her way, with a chance of just being missed by her, and having to meet the wash of her screws as she tore by us. We waited and she slowly swung round and revealed herself to us as a large steamer with all her portholes alight. I think the way those lights came slowly into view was one of the most wonderful things we shall ever see. It meant deliverance at once: that was the amazing thing to us all. We had thought of the afternoon as our time of rescue, and here only a few hours after the *Titanic* sank, before it was yet light, we were to be taken aboard. It seemed almost too good to be true, and I think everyone's eyes filled with tears, men's as well as women's, as they saw again the rows of lights one above the other shining kindly to them across the water, and 'Thank God!' was murmured in heartfelt tones round the boat. The boat swung round and the crew began their long row to the steamer; the captain called for a song and led off with 'Pull for the shore, boys.' The crew took it up quaveringly and the passengers joined in, but I think one verse was all they sang. It was too early yet, gratitude was too deep and sudden in its overwhelming intensity, for us to sing very steadily. Presently, finding the song had not gone very well, we tried a cheer, and that went better. It was more easy to relieve our feelings with a noise, and time and tune were not necessary ingredients in a cheer.

In the midst of our thankfulness for deliverance, one name was mentioned with the deepest feeling of gratitude: that of Marconi. I wish that he had been there to hear the chorus of gratitude that went out to him for the wonderful invention that spared us many hours, and perhaps many days, of wandering about the sea in hunger and storm and cold. Perhaps our gratitude was sufficiently intense and vivid to 'Marconi' some of it to him that night.

All around we saw boats making for the *Carpathia* and heard their shouts and cheers. Our crew rowed hard in friendly rivalry with other boats to be among the first home, but we must have been eighth or ninth at the side. We had a heavy load aboard, and had to row round a huge iceberg on the way.

And then, as if to make everything complete for our happiness, came the dawn. First a beautiful, quiet shimmer away in the east, then a soft golden glow that crept up stealthily from behind the skyline as if it were trying not to be noticed as it stole over the sea and spread itself quietly in every direction – so quietly, as if to make us believe it had been there all the time and we had not observed it. Then the sky turned faintly pink and in the distance the thinnest, fleeciest clouds stretched in thin bands across the horizon and close down to it, becoming every moment more and more pink. And next the stars died, slowly – save one which remained long after the others just above the horizon; and nearby, with the crescent turned to the north, and the lower horn just touching the horizon, the thinnest, palest of moons.

And with the dawn came a faint breeze from the west, the first breath of wind we had felt since the *Titanic* stopped her engines. Anticipating a few hours – as the day drew on to 8 a.m., the time the last boats came up – this breeze increased to a fresh wind which whipped up the sea, so that the last boat laden with people had an anxious time in the choppy waves before they reached the *Carpathia*. An officer remarked that one of the boats could not have stayed afloat another hour: the wind had held off just long enough.

The captain shouted along our boat to the crew, as they strained at the oars – two pulling and an extra one facing them and pushing to try to keep pace with the other boats – 'A new moon! Turn your money over, boys! That is, if you have any!' We laughed at him for the quaint superstition at such a time, and it was good to laugh again, but he showed his disbelief in another superstition when he added, 'Well, I shall never say again that 13 is an unlucky number. Boat 13 is the best friend we ever had.'

If there had been among us – and it is almost certain that there were, so fast does superstition cling – those who feared events connected with the number thirteen, I am certain they agreed with him, and never again will they attach any importance to such a foolish belief. Perhaps the belief itself will receive a shock when it is remembered that boat 13 of the *Titanic* brought away a full load from the sinking vessel, carried them in such comfort all night that they had not even a drop of water on them, and landed them safely at the *Carpathia*'s side, where they climbed aboard without a single mishap. It almost tempts one to be the thirteenth at table, or to choose a house numbered 13 fearless of any croaking about flying in the face of what is humorously called 'Providence'.

Looking towards the *Carpathia* in the faint light, we saw what seemed to be two large fully rigged sailing ships near the horizon, with all sails set, standing up near her, and we decided that they must be fishing vessels off the Banks of Newfoundland which had seen the *Carpathia* stop and were waiting to see if she wanted help of any kind. But in a few minutes more the light shone on them and they stood revealed as huge icebergs, peaked in a way that readily suggested a ship. When the sun rose higher, it turned them pink, and sinister as they looked towering like rugged white peaks of rock out of the sea, and terrible as was the disaster one of them had caused, there was an awful beauty about them which could not be overlooked. Later, when the sun came above the horizon, they sparkled and glittered in its rays; deadly white, like frozen snow rather than translucent ice.

As the dawn crept towards us there lay another almost directly in the line between our boat and the *Carpathia*, and a few minutes later, another on her port quarter, and more again on the southern and western horizons, as far as the eye could reach: all differing in shape and size and tones of colour according as the sun shone through them or was reflected directly or obliquely from them.

We drew near our rescuer and presently could discern the bands on her funnel, by which the crew could tell she was a Cunarder; and already some boats were at her side and passengers climbing up her ladders. We had to give the iceberg a wide berth and make a detour to the south: we knew it was sunk a long way below the surface with such things as projecting ledges – not that it was very likely there was one so near the surface as to endanger our small boat, but we were not inclined to take any risks for the sake of a few more minutes when safety lay so near.

Once clear of the berg, we could read the Cunarder's name – *C A R P A T H I A* – a name we are not likely ever to forget. We shall see her sometimes, perhaps, in the shipping lists – as I have done already once when she left Genoa on her return voyage – and the way her lights climbed up over the horizon in the darkness, the way she swung and showed her lighted portholes, and the moment when we read her name on her side will all come back in a flash; we shall live again the scene of rescue, and feel the same thrill of gratitude for all she brought us that night.

We rowed up to her about 4.30, and sheltering on the port side from the swell, held on by two ropes at the stern and bow. Women went up the side first, climbing rope ladders with a noose round their shoulders to help their ascent; men passengers scrambled next, and the crew last of all. The baby went up in a bag with the opening tied up: it had been quite well all the time, and never suffered any ill effects from its cold journey in the night. We set foot on deck with very thankful hearts, grateful beyond the possibility of adequate expression to feel a solid ship beneath us once more.

6

The Sinking of the *Titanic*,
Seen From Her Deck

The two preceding chapters have been to a large extent the narrative of a single eyewitness and an account of the escape of one boat only from the *Titanic*'s side. It will be well now to return to the *Titanic* and reconstruct a more general and complete account from the experiences of many people in different parts of the ship. A considerable part of these experiences was related to the writer first hand by survivors, both on board the *Carpathia* and at other times, but some are derived from other sources which are probably as accurate as first-hand information. Other reports, which seemed at first sight to have been founded on the testimony of eyewitnesses, have been found on examination to have passed through several hands, and have therefore been rejected. The testimony even of eyewitnesses has in some cases been excluded when it seemed not to agree with direct evidence of a number of other witnesses or with what reasoned judgement considered probable in the circumstances. In this category are the reports of explosions before the

Titanic sank, the breaking of the ship in two parts, the suicide of officers. It would be well to notice here that the *Titanic* was in her correct course, the southerly one, and in the position which prudence dictates as a safe one under the ordinary conditions at that time of the year: to be strictly accurate she was sixteen miles south of the regular summer route which all companies follow from January to August.

Perhaps the real history of the disaster should commence with the afternoon of Sunday, when Marconigrams were received by the *Titanic* from the ships ahead of her, warning her of the existence of icebergs. In connection with this must be taken the marked fall of temperature observed by everyone in the afternoon and evening of this day as well as the very low temperature of the water. These have generally been taken to indicate that without any possibility of doubt we were near an iceberg region, and the severest condemnation has been poured on the heads of the officers and captain for not having regard to these climatic conditions; but here caution is necessary. There can be little doubt now that the low temperature observed can be traced to the icebergs and ice-field subsequently encountered, but experienced sailors are aware that it might have been observed without any icebergs being near. The cold Labrador current sweeps down by Newfoundland across the track of Atlantic liners, but does not necessarily carry icebergs with it; cold winds blow from Greenland and Labrador and not always from icebergs and icefields. So that falls in temperature of sea and air are not prima facie evidence of the close proximity of icebergs. On the other hand, a single iceberg separated by many miles from its fellows might sink a ship, but certainly would not cause a drop in temperature either of the air or water. Then, as the Labrador current meets the warm Gulf Stream flowing from the Gulf of Mexico across to Europe, they do not necessarily intermingle, nor do they always run side by side or one on top of the other, but often interlaced, like the fingers of two hands. As a ship sails across this region the thermometer will record within a few miles temperatures of 34°, 58°, 35°, 59°, and so on.

It is little wonder then that sailors become accustomed to place little reliance on temperature conditions as a means of estimating the probabilities of encountering ice in their track. An experienced sailor has told me that nothing is more difficult to diagnose than the presence of icebergs, and a strong confirmation of this is found in the official sailing directions issued by the Hydrographic Department of the British Admiralty. 'No reliance can be placed on any warning being conveyed to the mariner, by a fall in temperature, either of sea or air, of approaching ice. Some decrease in temperature has occasionally been recorded, but more often none has been observed.'

But notification by Marconigram of the exact location of icebergs is a vastly different matter. I remember with deep feeling the effect this information had on us when it first became generally known on board the *Carpathia*. Rumours of it went round on Wednesday morning, grew to definite statements in the afternoon, and were confirmed when one of the *Titanic* officers admitted the truth of it in reply to a direct question. I shall never forget the overwhelming sense of hopelessness that came over some of us as we obtained definite knowledge of the warning messages. It was not then the unavoidable accident we had hitherto supposed: the sudden plunging into a region crowded with icebergs which no seaman, however skilled a navigator he might be, could have avoided! The beautiful *Titanic* wounded too deeply to recover, the cries of the drowning still ringing in our ears and the thousands of homes that mourned all these calamities – none of all these things need ever have been!

It is no exaggeration to say that men who went through all the experiences of the collision and the rescue and the subsequent scenes on the quay at New York with hardly a tremor, were quite overcome by this knowledge and turned away, unable to speak; I for one, did so, and I know others who told me they were similarly affected.

I think we all came to modify our opinions on this matter, however, when we learnt more of the general conditions attending transatlantic steamship services. The discussion as to who was responsible for these warnings being disregarded had perhaps better be postponed to a later chapter. One of these warnings was handed to Mr Ismay by Captain Smith at 5 p.m. and returned at the latter's request at 7 p.m., that it might be posted for the information of officers; as a result of the messages they were instructed to keep a special lookout for ice. This, Second Officer Lightoller did until he was relieved at 10 p.m. by First Officer Murdock, to whom he handed on the instructions. During Mr Lightoller's watch, about 9 p.m., the captain had joined him on the bridge and discussed 'the time we should be getting up towards the vicinity of the ice, and how we should recognise it if we should see it, and refreshing our minds on the indications that ice gives when it is in the vicinity'. Apparently, too, the officers had discussed among themselves the proximity of ice and Mr Lightoller had remarked that they would be approaching the position where ice had been reported during his watch. The lookouts were cautioned similarly, but no ice was sighted until a few minutes before the collision, when the lookout man saw the iceberg and rang the bell three times, the usual signal from the crow's nest when anything is seen dead ahead.

By telephone he reported to the bridge the presence of an iceberg, but Mr Murdock had already ordered Quartermaster Hichens at the wheel to starboard the helm, and the vessel began to swing away from the berg. But it was far too late at the speed she was going to hope to steer the huge Titanic, over a sixth of a mile long, out of reach of danger. Even if the iceberg had been visible half a mile away it is doubtful whether some portion of her tremendous length would not have been touched, and it is in the highest degree unlikely that the lookout could have seen the berg half a mile away in the conditions that existed that night, even with glasses. The very smoothness of the water made the presence of ice a more difficult matter to detect. In ordinary conditions the dash of the waves against the foot of an iceberg surrounds it with a circle of white foam visible for some distance, long before the iceberg itself; but here was an oily sea sweeping smoothly round the deadly monster and causing no indication of its presence.

There is little doubt, moreover, that the crow's nest is not a good place from which to detect icebergs. It is proverbial that they adopt to a large extent the colour of their surroundings; and seen from above at a high angle, with the black, foam-free sea behind, the iceberg must have been almost invisible until the *Titanic* was close upon it. I was much struck by a remark of Sir Ernest Shackleton on his method of detecting icebergs – to place a lookout man as low down near the waterline as he could get him. Remembering how we had watched the *Titanic* with all her lights out, standing upright like 'an enormous black finger', as one observer stated, and had only seen her thus because she loomed black against the sky behind her, I saw at once how much better the sky was than the black sea to show up an iceberg's bulk.

And so in a few moments the *Titanic* had run obliquely on the berg, and with a shock that was astonishingly slight – so slight that many passengers never noticed it – the submerged portion of the berg had cut her open on the starboard side in the most vulnerable portion of her anatomy – the bilge. The most authentic accounts say that the wound began at about the location of the foremast and extended far back to the stern, the brunt of the blow being taken by the forward plates, which were either punctured through both bottoms directly by the blow, or through one skin only, and as this was torn away it ripped out some of the inner plates. The fact that she went down by the head shows that probably only the forward plates were doubly punctured, the stern ones being cut open through the outer skin only. After the collision, Murdock had at once reversed the engines and brought the ship to a standstill, but the iceberg had floated away astern. The shock, though little felt by the enormous mass of the ship, was sufficient to dislodge a large quantity of ice from the berg: the forecastle deck was found to be covered with pieces of ice.

Feeling the shock, Captain Smith rushed out of his cabin to the bridge, and in reply to his anxious enquiry was told by Murdock that ice had been struck and the emergency doors instantly closed. The officers roused by the collision went on deck: some to the bridge; others, while hearing nothing of the extent of the damage, saw no necessity for doing so. Captain Smith at once sent the carpenter below to sound the ship, and Fourth Officer Boxhall to the steerage to report damage. The latter found there a very dangerous condition of things and reported to Captain Smith, who then sent him to the mail room; and here again, it was easy to see, matters looked very serious. Mail bags were floating about and the water rising rapidly. All this was reported to the captain, who ordered the lifeboats to be got ready at once. Mr Boxhall went to the chartroom to work out the ship's position, which he then handed to the Marconi operators for transmission to any ship near enough to help in the work of rescue.

Reports of the damage done were by this time coming to the captain from many quarters, from the chief engineer, from the designer – Mr Andrews – and in a dramatic way from the sudden appearance on deck of a swarm of stokers who had rushed up from below as the water poured into the boiler rooms and coal bunkers: they were immediately ordered down below to duty again. Realising the urgent heed of help, he went personally to the Marconi room and gave orders to the operators to get into touch with all the ships they could and to tell them to come quickly. The assistant operator Bride had been asleep, and knew of the damage only when Phillips, in charge of the Marconi room, told him ice had been encountered. They started to send out the well-known 'CQD' message – which interpreted means: CQ 'all stations at tend,' and D, 'distress', the position of the vessel in latitude and longitude following. Later, they sent out 'SOS', an arbitrary message agreed upon as an international code-signal.

Soon after the vessel struck, Mr Ismay had learnt of the nature of the accident from the captain and chief engineer, and after dressing and going on deck had spoken to some of the officers not yet thoroughly acquainted with the grave injury done to the vessel. By this time all those in any way connected with the management and navigation must have known the importance of making use of all the ways of safety known to them – and that without any delay. That they thought at first that the *Titanic* would sink as soon as she did is doubtful; but probably as the reports came in they knew that her ultimate loss in a few hours was a likely contingency. On the other hand, there is evidence that some of the officers in charge of boats quite expected the embarkation was a precautionary measure and they would all return after daylight. Certainly the first information that ice had been struck conveyed to those in charge no sense of the gravity of the circumstances: one officer even retired to his cabin and another advised a steward to go back to his berth as there was no danger.

And so the order was sent round, 'All passengers on deck with lifebelts on'; and in obedience to this a crowd of hastily dressed or partially dressed people began to assemble on the decks belonging to their respective classes (except the steerage passengers who were allowed access to other decks), tying on lifebelts over their clothing. In some parts of the ship women were separated from the men and assembled together near the boats, in others men and women mingled freely together, husbands helping their own wives and families and then other women and children into the boats. The officers spread themselves about the decks, superintending the work of lowering and loading the boats, and in three cases were ordered by their superior officers to take charge of them. At this stage great difficulty was experienced in getting women to leave the ship, especially where the order was so rigorously enforced, 'Women and children only.' Women in many cases refused to leave their husbands, and were actually forcibly lifted up and dropped in the boats. They argued with the officers, demanding reasons, and in some cases even when induced to get in were disposed to think the whole thing a joke, or a precaution which it seemed to them rather foolish to take. In this they were encouraged by the men left behind, who, in the same condition of ignorance, said goodbye to their friends as they went down, adding that they would see them again at breakfast-time. To illustrate further how little danger was apprehended – when it was discovered on the first class deck that the forward lower deck was covered with small ice, snowballing matches were arranged for the following morning, and some passengers even went down to the deck and brought back small pieces of ice which were handed round.

Below decks too was additional evidence that no one thought of immediate danger. Two ladies walking along one of the corridors came across a group of people gathered round a door which they were trying vainly to open, and on the other side of which a man was demanding in loud terms to be let out. Either his door was locked and the key not to be found, or the collision had jammed the lock and prevented the key from turning. The ladies thought he must be afflicted in some way to make such a noise, but one of the men was assuring him that in no circumstances should he be left, and that his (the bystander's) son would be along soon and would smash down his door if it was not opened in the mean time. 'He has a stronger arm than I have,' he added. The son arrived presently and proceeded to make short work of the door: it was smashed in and the inmate released, to his great satisfaction and with many expressions of gratitude to his rescuer. But one of the head stewards who came up at this juncture was so incensed at the damage done to the property of his company, and so little aware of the infinitely greater damage done the ship, that he warned the man who had released the prisoner that he would be arrested on arrival in New York.

It must be borne in mind that no general warning had been issued to passengers: here and there were experienced travellers to whom collision with an iceberg was sufficient to cause them to make every preparation for leaving the ship, but the great majority were never enlightened as to the amount of damage done, or even as to what had happened. We knew in a vague way that we had collided with an iceberg, but there our knowledge ended, and most of us drew no deductions from that fact alone. Another factor that prevented some from taking to the boats was the drop to the water below and the journey into the unknown sea: certainly it looked a tremendous way down in the darkness, the sea and the night both seemed very cold and lonely; and here was the ship, so firm and well lighted and warm.

But perhaps what made so many people declare their decision to remain was their strong belief in the theory of the *Titanic*'s unsinkable construction. Again and again was it repeated, 'This ship cannot sink; it is only a question of waiting until another ship comes up and takes us off.' Husbands expected to follow their wives and join them either in

New York or by transfer in mid-ocean from steamer to steamer. Many passengers relate that they were told by officers that the ship was a lifeboat and could not go down; one lady affirms that the captain told her the *Titanic* could not sink for two or three days; no doubt this was immediately after the collision.

It is not any wonder, then, that many elected to remain, deliberately choosing the deck of the *Titanic* to a place in a lifeboat. And yet the boats had to go down, and so at first they went half full: this is the real explanation of why they were not as fully loaded as the later ones. It is important then to consider the question how far the captain was justified in withholding all the knowledge he had from every passenger. From one point of view he should have said to them, 'This ship will sink in a few hours: there are the boats, and only women and children can go to them.' But had he the authority to enforce such an order? There are such things as panics and rushes which get beyond the control of a handful of officers, even if armed, and where even the bravest of men get swept off their feet – mentally as well as physically.

On the other hand, if he decided to withhold all definite knowledge of danger from all passengers and at the same time persuade – and if it was not sufficient, compel – women and children to take to the boats, it might result in their all being saved. He could not foresee the tenacity of their faith in the boat: there is ample evidence that he left the bridge when the ship had come to rest and went among passengers urging them to get into the boat and rigorously excluding all but women and children. Some would not go. Officer Lowe testified that he shouted, 'Who's next for the boat?' and could get no replies. The boats even were sent away half-loaded – although the fear of their buckling in the middle was responsible as well for this – but the captain with the few boats at his disposal could hardly do more than persuade and advise in the terrible circumstances in which he was placed.

How appalling to think that with a few more boats – and the ship was provided with that particular kind of davit that would launch more boats – there would have been no decision of that kind to make! It could have been stated plainly: 'This ship will sink in a few hours: there is room in the boats for all passengers, beginning with women and children.'

Poor Captain Smith! I care not whether the responsibility for such speed in iceberg regions will rest on his shoulders or not: no man ever had to make such a choice as he had that night, and it seems difficult to see how he can be blamed for withholding from passengers such information as he had of the danger that was imminent.

When one reads in the press that lifeboats arrived at the *Carpathia* half full, it seems at first sight a dreadful thing that this should have been allowed to happen; but it is so easy to make these criticisms afterwards, so easy to say that Captain Smith should have told everyone of the condition of the vessel. He was faced with many conditions that night which such criticism overlooks. Let any fair-minded person consider some few of the problems presented to him – the ship was bound to sink in a few hours; there was lifeboat accommodation for all women and children and some men; there was no way of getting some women to go except by telling them the ship was doomed, a course he deemed it best not to take; and he knew the danger of boats buckling when loaded full. His solution of these problems was apparently the following: to send the boats down half full, with such women as would go, and to tell the boats to stand by to pick up more passengers passed down from the cargo ports. There is good evidence that this was part of the plan: I heard an officer give the order to four boats and a lady in number 4 boat on the port side tells me the sailors were so long looking for the port where the captain personally had told them to wait, that they were in danger of being sucked under by the vessel. How far any systematic attempt was made to stand by the ports, I do not know: I never saw one open or any boat standing near on the starboard side; but then, boats 9 to 15 went down full, and on reaching the sea rowed away at once. There is good evidence, then, that Captain Smith fully intended to load the boats full in this way. The failure to carry out the intention is one of the things the whole world regrets, but consider again the great size of the ship and the short time to make decisions, and the omission is more easily understood. The fact is that such a contingency as lowering away boats was not even considered beforehand, and there is much cause for gratitude that as many as seven hundred and five people were rescued. The whole question of a captain's duties seems to require revision. It was totally impossible for any one man to attempt to control the ship that night, and the weather conditions could not well have been more favourable for doing so. One of the reforms that seem inevitable is that one man shall be responsible for the boats, their manning, loading and lowering, leaving the captain free to be on the bridge to the last moment.

But to return for a time to the means taken to attract the notice of other ships. The wireless operators were now in touch with several ships, and calling to them to come quickly for the water was pouring in and the *Titanic* beginning to go down by the head. Bride testified that the first reply received was from a German boat, the *Frankfurt*, which was 'All right: stand by', but not giving her position. From comparison of the strength of signals received from the *Frankfurt* and from other boats, the operators estimated the *Frankfurt* was the nearest; but subsequent events proved that this was not so. She was, in fact, one hundred and forty miles away and arrived at 10.50 a.m. next morning, when the *Carpathia* had left with the rescued. The next reply was from the *Carpathia*, fifty-eight miles away on the outbound route to the Mediterranean, and it was a prompt and welcome one – 'Coming hard', followed by the position. Then followed the *Olympic*, and with her they talked for some time, but she was five hundred and sixty miles away on the southern route, too far to be of any immediate help. At the speed of 23 knots she would expect to be up about 1 p.m. next day, and this was about the time that those in boat 13 had calculated. We had always assumed in the boat that the stokers who gave this information had it from one of the officers before they left; but in the absence of any knowledge of the much nearer ship, the *Carpathia*, it is more probable that they knew in a general way where the sister ship, the *Olympic*, should be, and had made a rough calculation.

Other ships in touch by wireless were the *Mount Temple*, fifty miles; the *Birma*, one hundred miles; the *Parisian*, one hundred and fifty miles; the *Virginian*, one hundred and fifty miles; and the *Baltic*, three hundred miles. But closer than any of these – closer even than the *Carpathia* – were two ships: the *Californian*, less than twenty miles away, with the wireless operator off duty and unable to catch the 'CQD' signal which was now making the air for many miles around quiver in its appeal for help – immediate, urgent help – for the hundreds of people who stood on the *Titanic's* deck.

The second vessel was a small steamer some few miles ahead on the port side, without any wireless apparatus, her name and destination still unknown; and yet the evidence for her presence that night seems too strong to be disregarded. Mr Boxhall states that he and Captain Smith saw her quite plainly some five miles away, and could distinguish the masthead lights and a red port light. They at once hailed her with rockets and Morse electric signals, to which Boxhall saw no reply, but Captain Smith and stewards affirmed they did. The second and third officers saw the signals sent and her lights, the latter from the lifeboat of which he was in charge. Seaman Hopkins testified that he was told by the captain to row for the light; and we in boat 13 certainly saw it in the same position and rowed towards it for some time. But notwithstanding all the efforts made to attract its attention, it drew slowly away and the lights sank below the horizon.

The pity of it! So near, and so many people waiting for the shelter its decks could have given so easily. It seems impossible to think that this ship ever replied to the signals: those who said so must have been mistaken. The United States Senate Committee in its report does not hesitate to say that this unknown steamer and the *Californian* are identical, and that the failure on the part of the latter to come to the help of the *Titanic* is culpable negligence. There is undoubted evidence that some of the crew on the *Californian* saw our rockets; but it seems impossible to believe that the captain and officers knew of our distress and deliberately ignored it. Judgement on the matter had better be suspended until further information is forthcoming. An engineer who has served in the transatlantic service tells me that it is a common practice for small boats to leave the fishing smacks to which they belong and row away for miles; sometimes even being lost and wandering about among icebergs, and even not being found again. In these circumstances, rockets are part of a fishing smack's equipment, and are sent up to indicate to the small boats how to return. Is it conceivable that the *Californian* thought our rockets were such signals, and therefore paid no attention to them?

Incidentally, this engineer did not hesitate to add that it is doubtful if a big liner would stop to help a small fishing boat sending off distress signals, or even would turn about to help one which she herself had cut down as it lay in her path without a light. He was strong in his affirmation that such things were commonly known to all officers in the transatlantic service.

With regard to the other vessels in wireless communication, the *Mount Temple* was the only one near enough from the point of distance to have arrived in time to be of help, but between her and the *Titanic* lay the enormous ice-floe, and icebergs were near her in addition.

The seven ships which caught the message started at once to her help but were all stopped on the way (except the *Birma*) by the *Carpathia*'s wireless announcing the fate of the *Titanic* and the people aboard her. The message must have affected the captains of these ships very deeply: they would understand far better than the travelling public what it meant to lose such a beautiful ship on her first voyage.

The only thing now left to be done was to get the lifeboats away as quickly as possible, and to this task the other officers were in the meantime devoting all their endeavours. Mr Lightoller sent away boat after boat: in one he had put twenty-four women and children, in another thirty, in another thirty-five; and then, running short of seamen to man the boats he sent Major Peuchen, an expert yachtsman, in the next, to help with its navigation. By the time these had been filled, he had difficulty in finding women for the fifth and sixth boats for the reasons already stated. All this time the passengers remained – to use his own expression – 'as quiet as if in church'. To man and supervise the loading of six boats must have taken him nearly up to the time of the *Titanic*'s sinking, taking an average of some twenty minutes to a boat. Still at work to the end, he remained on the ship till she sank and went down with her. His evidence before the United States Committee was as follows: 'Did you leave the ship?' 'No, sir.' 'Did the ship leave you?' 'Yes, sir.'

It was a piece of work well and cleanly done, and his escape from the ship, one of the most wonderful of all, seems almost a reward for his devotion to duty.

Captain Smith, Officers Wilde and Murdock were similarly engaged in other parts of the ship, urging women to get in the boats, in some cases directing junior officers to go down in some of them – Officers Pitman, Boxhall, and Lowe were sent in this way – in others placing members of the crew in charge. As the boats were lowered, orders were shouted to them where to make for: some were told to stand by and wait for further instructions, others to row for the light of the disappearing steamer.

It is a pitiful thing to recall the effects of sending down the first boats half full. In some cases men in the company of their wives had actually taken seats in the boats – young men, married only a few weeks and on their wedding trip – and had done so only because no more women could then be found; but the strict interpretation by the particular officer in charge there of the rule of 'Women and children only', compelled them to get out again. Some of these boats were lowered and reached the *Carpathia* with many vacant seats. The anguish of the young wives in such circumstances can only be imagined. In other parts of the ship, however, a different interpretation was placed on the rule, and men were allowed and even invited by officers to get in – not only to form part of the crew, but even as passengers. This, of course, in the first boats and when no more women could be found.

The varied understanding of this rule was a frequent subject of discussion on the *Carpathia* – in fact, the rule itself was debated with much heart-searching. There were not wanting many who doubted the justice of its rigid enforcement, who could not think it well that a husband should be separated from his wife and family, leaving them penniless, or a young bridegroom from his wife of a few short weeks, while ladies with few relatives, with no one dependent upon them, and few responsibilities of any kind, were saved. It was mostly these ladies who pressed this view, and even men seemed to think there was a good deal to be said for it. Perhaps there is, theoretically, but it would be impossible, I think, in practice. To quote Mr Lightoller again in his evidence before the United States Senate Committee – when asked if it was a rule of the sea that women and children be saved first, he replied, 'No, it is a rule of human nature.' That is no doubt the real reason for its existence.

But the selective process of circumstances brought about results that were very bitter to some. It was heartrending for ladies who had lost all they held dearest in the world to hear that in one boat was a stoker picked up out of the sea so drunk that he stood up and brandished his arms about, and had to be thrown down by ladies and sat upon to keep him quiet. If comparisons can be drawn, it did seem better that an educated, refined man should be saved than one who had flown to drink as his refuge in time of danger.

These discussions turned sometimes to the old enquiry – 'What is the purpose of all this? Why the disaster? Why this man saved and that man lost? Who has arranged that my husband should live a few short happy years in the world, and the happiest days in those years with me these last few weeks, and then be taken from me?' I heard no one attribute all this to a Divine Power who ordains and arranges the lives of men, and as part of a definite scheme sends such calamity and misery in order to purify, to teach, to spiritualise. I do not say there were not people who thought and said they saw Divine Wisdom in it all, so inscrutable that we in our ignorance saw it not; but I did not hear it expressed, and this book is intended to be no more than a partial chronicle of the many different experiences and convictions.

There were those, on the other hand, who did not fail to say emphatically that indifference to the rights and feelings of others, blindness to duty towards our fellow men and women, was in the last analysis the cause of most of the human misery in the world. And it should undoubtedly appeal more to our sense of justice to attribute these things to our own lack of consideration for others than to shift the responsibility on to a Power whom we first postulate as being All-wise and All-loving.

All the boats were lowered and sent away by about 2 a.m., and by this time the ship was very low in the water, the forecastle deck completely submerged, and the sea creeping steadily up to the bridge and probably only a few yards away.

No one on the ship can have had any doubt now as to her ultimate fate, and yet the fifteen hundred passengers and crew on board made no demonstration, and not a sound came from them as they stood quietly on the decks or went about their duties below. It seems incredible, and yet if it was a continuation of the same feeling that existed on deck before the boats left – and I have no doubt it was – the explanation is straightforward and reasonable in its simplicity. An attempt is made in the last chapter to show why the attitude of the crowd was so quietly courageous. There are accounts which picture excited crowds running about the deck in terror, fighting and struggling, but two of the most accurate observers, Colonel Gracie and Mr Lightoller, affirm that this was not so, that absolute order and quietness prevailed. The band still played to cheer the hearts of all near; the engineers and their crew – I have never heard anyone speak of a single engineer being seen on deck – still worked at the electric light engines, far away below, keeping them going until no human being could do so a second longer, right until the ship tilted on end and the engines broke loose and fell down. The light failed then only because the engines were no longer there to produce light, not because the men who worked them were not standing by them to do their duty. To be down in the bowels of the ship, far away from the deck where at any rate there was a chance of a dive and a swim and a possible rescue; to know that when the ship went – as they knew it must soon – there could be no possible hope of climbing up in time to reach the sea; to know all these things and yet to keep the engines going that the decks might be lighted to the last moment, required sublime courage.

But this courage is required of every engineer and it is not called by that name: it is called 'duty'. To stand by his engines to the last possible moment is his duty. There could be no better example of the supremest courage being but duty well done than to remember the engineers of the *Titanic* still at work as she heeled over and flung them with their engines down the length of the ship. The simple statement that the lights kept on to the last is really their epitaph, but Lowell's words would seem to apply to them with peculiar force:

> The longer on this earth we live
> And weigh the various qualities of men –
> The more we feel the high, stern-featured beauty
> Of plain devotedness to duty.
> Steadfast and still, nor paid with mortal praise,
> But finding amplest recompense
> For life's ungarlanded expense
> In work done squarely and unwasted days.

For some time before she sank, the *Titanic* had a considerable list to port, so much so that one boat at any rate swung so far away from the side that difficulty was experienced in getting passengers in. This list was increased towards the end, and Colonel Gracie relates that Mr Lightoller, who has a deep, powerful voice, ordered all passengers to the starboard side. This was close before the end. They crossed over, and as they did so a crowd of steerage passengers rushed up and filled the decks so full that there was barely room to move. Soon afterwards the great vessel swung slowly, stern in the air, the lights went out, and while some were flung into the water and others dived off, the great majority still clung to the rails, to the sides and roofs of deck-structures, lying prone on the deck. And in this position they were when, a few minutes later, the enormous vessel dived obliquely downwards. As she went, no doubt many still clung to the rails, but most would do their best to get away from her and jump as she slid forwards and downwards. Whatever they did, there can be little question that most of them would be taken down by suction, to come up again a few moments later and to fill the air with those heartrending cries which fell on the ears of those in the lifeboats with such amazement. Another survivor, on the other hand, relates that he had dived from the stern before she heeled over, and swam round under her enormous triple screws lifted by now high out of the water as she stood on end. Fascinated by the extraordinary sight, he watched them up above his head, but presently realising the necessity of getting away as quickly as possible, he started to swim from the ship, but as he did she dived forward, the screws passing near his head. His experience is that not only was no suction present, but even a wave was created which washed him away from the place where she had gone down.

Of all those fifteen hundred people, flung into the sea as the *Titanic* went down, innocent victims of thoughtlessness and apathy of those responsible for their safety, only a very few found their way to the *Carpathia*. It will serve no good purpose to dwell any longer on the scene of helpless men and women struggling in the water. The heart of everyone who has read of their helplessness has gone out to them in deepest love and sympathy; and the knowledge that their struggle in the water was in most cases short and not physically painful because of the low temperature – the evidence seems to show that few lost their lives by drowning – is some consolation.

If everyone sees to it that his sympathy with them is so practical as to force him to follow up the question of reforms personally, not leaving it to experts alone, then he will have at any rate done something to atone for the loss of so many valuable lives.

We had now better follow the adventures of those who were rescued from the final event in the disaster. Two accounts – those of Colonel Gracie and Mr Lightoller – agree very closely. The former went down clinging to a rail, the latter dived before the ship went right under, but was sucked down and held against one of the blowers. They were both carried down for what seemed a long distance, but Mr Lightoller was finally blown up again by a 'terrific gust' that came up the blower and forced him clear. Colonel Gracie came to the surface after holding his breath for what seemed an eternity, and they both swam about holding on to any wreckage they could find. Finally they saw an upturned collapsible boat and climbed on it in company with twenty other men, among them Bride, the Marconi operator. After remaining thus for some hours, with the sea washing them to the waist, they stood up as day broke, in two rows, back to back, balancing themselves as well as they could, and afraid to turn lest the boat should roll over. Finally a lifeboat saw them and took them off, an operation attended with the greatest difficulty, and they reached the *Carpathia* in the early dawn. Not many people have gone through such an experience as those men did, lying all night on an overturned, ill-balanced boat, and praying together, as they did all the time, for the day and a ship to take them off.

Some account must now be attempted of the journey of the fleet of boats to the *Carpathia*, but it must necessarily be very brief. Experiences differed considerably: some had no encounters at all with icebergs, no lack of men to row, discovered lights and food and water, were picked up after only a few hours' exposure, and suffered very little discomfort; others seemed to see icebergs round them all night long and to be always rowing round them; others had so few men aboard – in some cases only two or three – that ladies had to row and in one case to steer, found no lights, food or water, and were adrift many hours, in some cases nearly eight.

The first boat to be picked up by the *Carpathia* was one in charge of Mr Boxhall. There was only one other man rowing and ladies worked at the oars. A green light burning in this boat all night was the greatest comfort to the rest of us who had nothing to steer by: although it meant little in the way of safety in itself, it was a point to which we could look. The green light was the first intimation Captain Rostron had of our position, and he steered for it and picked up its passengers first.

Mr Pitman was sent by First Officer Murdock in charge of boat 5, with forty passengers and five of the crew. It would have held more, but no women could be found at the time it was lowered. Mr Pitman says that after leaving the ship he felt confident she would float and they would all return. A passenger in this boat relates that men could not be induced to embark when she went down, and made appointments for the next morning with him. Tied to boat 5 was boat 7, one of those that contained few people: a few were transferred from number 5, but it would have held many more.

Fifth Officer Lowe was in charge of boat 14, with fifty-five women and children, and some of the crew. So full was the boat that as she went down Mr Lowe had to fire his revolver along the ship's side to prevent any more climbing in and causing her to buckle. This boat, like boat 13, was difficult to release from the lowering tackle, and had to be cut away after reaching the sea. Mr Lowe took in charge four other boats, tied them together with lines, found some of them not full, and transferred all his passengers to these, distributing them in the darkness as well as he could. Then returning to the place where the *Titanic* had sunk, he picked up some of those swimming in the water and went back to the four boats. On the way to the *Carpathia* he encountered one of the collapsible boats, and took aboard all those in her, as she seemed to be sinking.

Boat 12 was one of the four tied together, and the seaman in charge testified that he tried to row to the drowning, but with forty women and children and only one other man to row, it was not possible to pull such a heavy boat to the scene of the wreck.

Boat 2 was a small ship's boat and had four or five passengers and seven of the crew.

Boat 4 was one of the last to leave on the port side, and by this time there was such a list that deck chairs had to bridge the gap between the boat and the deck. When lowered, it remained for some time still attached to the ropes, and as the *Titanic* was rapidly sinking it seemed she would be pulled under. The boat was full of women, who besought the sailors to leave the ship, but in obedience to orders from the captain to stand by the cargo port, they remained near; so near, in fact, that they heard china falling and smashing as the ship went down by the head, and were nearly hit by wreckage thrown overboard by some of the officers and crew and intended to serve as rafts. They got clear finally, and were only a short distance away when the ship sank, so that they were able to pull some men aboard as they came to the surface.

This boat had an unpleasant experience in the night with icebergs; many were seen and avoided with difficulty.

Quartermaster Hichens was in charge of boat 6, and in the absence of sailors Major Peuchen was sent to help to man her. They were told to make for the light of the steamer seen on the port side, and followed it until it disappeared. There were forty women and children here.

Boat 8 had only one seaman, and as Captain Smith had enforced the rule of 'Women and children only', ladies had to row. Later in the night, when little progress had been made, the seaman took an oar and put a lady in charge of the tiller. This boat again was in the midst of icebergs.

Of the four collapsible boats – although collapsible is not really the correct term, for only a small portion collapses, the canvas edge; 'surf boats' is really their name – one was launched at the last moment by being pushed over as the sea rose to the edge of the deck, and was never righted. This is the one twenty men climbed on. Another was caught up by Mr Lowe and the passengers transferred, with the exception of three men who had perished from the effects of immersion. The boat was allowed to drift away and was found more than a month later by the *Celtic* in just the same condition. It is interesting to note how long this boat had remained afloat after she was supposed to be no longer seaworthy. A curious coincidence arose from the fact that one of my brothers happened to be travelling on the *Celtic*, and looking over the side, saw adrift on the sea a boat belonging to the *Titanic* in which I had been wrecked.

The two other collapsible boats came to the *Carpathia* carrying full loads of passengers: in one, the forward starboard boat and one of the last to leave, was Mr Ismay. Here four Chinamen were concealed under the feet of the passengers. How they got there no one knew – or indeed how they happened to be on the *Titanic*, for by the immigration laws of the United States they are not allowed to enter her ports.

It must be said, in conclusion, that there is the greatest cause for gratitude that all the boats launched carried their passengers safely to the rescue ship. It would not be right to accept this fact without calling attention to it: it would be easy to enumerate many things which might have been present as elements of danger.

But at the same time, one question recurs constantly to thought, and seems to call instantly for some reply.

Was it not possible during the three and a half hours that elapsed between the collision and the foundering to construct some kind of raft, sufficiently substantial to keep some of the passengers afloat?

The captain certainly knew such a raft would be urgently needed: it would seem to have been possible to tear up the decks and lash the planks to tables, wardrobes, deckchairs, etc.

But the only men who could really undertake such work – the sailors – were far too few even to lower and man the boats: not one of them could be spared for making rafts.

Again, perhaps the very tools with which such work would be carried out were in those parts of the hold which were from the first flooded with water. Perhaps these are the answers to a question which must have been asked hundreds of times.

7

The *Carpathia's* Return to New York

The journey of the *Carpathia* from the time she caught the 'CQD' from the *Titanic* at about 12.30 a.m. on Monday morning and turned swiftly about to her rescue, until she arrived at New York on the following Thursday at 8.30 p.m. was one that demanded of the captain, officers and crew of the vessel the most exact knowledge of navigation, the utmost vigilance in every department both before and after the rescue, and a capacity for organisation that must sometimes have been taxed to the breaking point.

The extent to which all these qualities were found present and the manner in which they were exercised stands to the everlasting credit of the Cunard Line and those of its servants who were in charge of the *Carpathia*. Captain Rostron's part in all this is a great one, and wrapped up though his action is in a modesty that is conspicuous in its nobility, it stands out even in his own account as a piece of work well and courageously done.

As soon as the *Titanic* called for help and gave her position, the *Carpathia* was turned and headed north: all hands were called on duty, a new watch of stokers was put on, and the highest speed of which she was capable was demanded of the engineers, with the result that the distance of fifty-eight miles between the two ships was covered in three and a half hours, a speed well beyond her normal capacity. The three doctors on board each took charge of a saloon, in readiness to render help to any who needed their services, the stewards and catering staff were hard at work preparing hot drinks and meals, and the purser's staff ready with blankets and berths for the shipwrecked passengers as soon as they got on board. On deck the sailors got ready lifeboats, swung them out on the davits, and stood by, prepared to lower away their crews if necessary; fixed rope ladders, cradle-chairs, nooses, and bags for the children at the hatches, to haul the rescued up the side. On the bridge was the captain with his officers, peering into the darkness eagerly to catch the first signs of the crippled *Titanic*, hoping, in spite of her last despairing message of 'Sinking by the head', to find her still afloat when her position was reached. A double watch of lookout men was set, for there were other things as well as the *Titanic* to look for that night, and soon they found them. As Captain Rostron said in his evidence, they saw icebergs on either side of them between 2.45 and 4 a.m., passing twenty large ones, one hundred to two hundred feet high, and many smaller ones, and 'frequently had to manoeuvre the ship to avoid them'. It was a time when every faculty was called upon for the highest use of which it was capable. With the knowledge before them that the enormous *Titanic*, the supposedly unsinkable ship, had struck ice and was sinking rapidly; with the lookout constantly calling to the bridge, as he must have done, 'Icebergs on the starboard', 'Icebergs on the port', it required courage and judgement beyond the ordinary to drive the ship ahead through that lane of icebergs and 'manoeuvre round them'. As he himself said, he 'took the risk of full speed in his desire to save life, and probably some people might blame him for taking such a risk'. But the Senate Committee assured him that they, at any rate, would not, and we of the lifeboats have certainly no desire to do so.

The ship was finally stopped at 4 a.m., with an iceberg reported dead ahead (the same no doubt we had to row around in boat 13 as we approached the *Carpathia*), and about the same time the first lifeboat was sighted. Again she had to be manoeuvred round the iceberg to pick up the boat, which was the one in charge of Mr Boxhall. From him the captain learned that the *Titanic* had gone down, and that he was too late to save anyone but those in lifeboats, which he could now see drawing up from every part of the horizon. Meanwhile, the passengers of the *Carpathia*, some of them aroused by the unusual vibration of the screw, some by sailors tramping overhead as they swung away the lifeboats and got ropes and lowering tackle ready, were beginning to come on deck just as day broke; and here an extraordinary sight met their eyes. As far as the eye could reach to the north and west lay an unbroken stretch of field ice, with icebergs still attached to the floe and rearing aloft their mass as a hill might suddenly rise from a level plain. Ahead and to the south and east huge floating monsters were showing up through the waning darkness, their number added to moment by moment as the dawn broke and flushed the horizon pink. It is remarkable how 'busy' all those icebergs made the sea look: to have gone to bed with nothing but sea and sky and to come on deck to find so many objects in sight made quite a change in the character of the sea: it looked quite crowded; and a lifeboat alongside and people clambering aboard, mostly women, in nightdresses and dressing gowns, in cloaks and shawls, in anything but ordinary clothes! Out ahead and on all sides little torches glittered faintly for a few moments and then guttered out – and shouts and cheers floated across the quiet sea. It would be difficult to imagine a more unexpected sight than this that lay before the *Carpathia*'s passengers as they lined the sides that morning in the early dawn.

No novelist would dare to picture such an array of beautiful climatic conditions – the rosy dawn, the morning star, the moon on the horizon, the sea stretching in level beauty to the skyline – and on this sea to place an icefield like the Arctic regions and icebergs in numbers everywhere – white and turning pink and deadly cold – and near them, rowing round the icebergs to avoid them, little boats coming suddenly out of mid-ocean, with passengers rescued from the most wonderful ship the world has known. No artist would have conceived such a picture: it would have seemed so highly dramatic as to border on the impossible, and would not have been attempted. Such a combination of events would pass the limit permitted the imagination of both author and artist.

The passengers crowded the rails and looked down at us as we rowed up in the early morning; stood quietly aside while the crew at the gangways below took us aboard, and watched us as if the ship had been in dock and we had rowed up to join her in a somewhat unusual way. Some of them have related that we were very quiet as we came aboard: it is quite true, we were; but so were they. There was very little excitement on either side: just the quiet demeanour of people who are in the presence of something too big as yet to lie within their mental grasp, and which they cannot yet discuss. And so they asked us politely to have hot coffee, which we did; and food, which we generally declined – we were not hungry – and they said very little at first about the lost *Titanic* and our adventures in the night.

Much that is exaggerated and false has been written about the mental condition of passengers as they came aboard: we have been described as being too dazed to understand what was happening, as being too overwhelmed to speak, and as looking before us with 'set, staring gaze', 'dazed with the shadow of the dread event'. That is, no doubt, what most people would expect in the circumstances, but I know it does not give a faithful record of how we did arrive: in fact it is simply not true. As remarked before, the one thing that matters in describing an event of this kind is the exact truth, as near as the fallible human mind can state it; and my own impression of our mental condition is that of supreme gratitude and relief at treading the firm decks of a ship again. I am aware that experiences differed considerably according to the boats occupied; that those who were uncertain of the fate of their relatives and friends had much to make them anxious and troubled; and that it is not possible to look into another person's consciousness and say what is written there; but dealing with mental conditions as far as they are delineated by facial and bodily expressions, I think joy, relief, gratitude were the dominant emotions written on the faces of those who climbed the rope ladders and were hauled up in cradles.

It must not be forgotten that no one in any one boat knew who were saved in other boats: few knew even how many boats there were and how many passengers could be saved. It was at the time probable that friends would follow them to the *Carpathia*, or be found on other steamers, or even on the pier at which we landed. The hysterical scenes that have been described are imaginative; true, one woman did fill the saloon with hysterical cries immediately after coming aboard, but she could not have known for a certainty that any of her friends were lost: probably the sense of relief after some hours of journeying about the sea was too much for her for a time.

One of the first things we did was to crowd round a steward with a bundle of telegraph forms. He was the bearer of the welcome news that passengers might send Marconigrams to their relatives free of charge, and soon he bore away the first sheaf of hastily scribbled messages to the operator; by the time the last boatload was aboard, the pile must have risen high in the Marconi cabin. We learned afterwards that many of these never reached their destination; and this is not a matter for surprise. There was only one operator – Cottam – on board, and although he was assisted to some extent later, when Bride from the *Titanic* had recovered from his injuries sufficiently to work the apparatus, he had so much to do that he fell asleep over this work on Tuesday night after three days' continuous duty without rest. But we did not know the messages were held back, and imagined our friends were aware of our safety; then, too, a roll call of the rescued was held in the *Carpathia*'s saloon on the Monday, and this was Marconied to land in advance of all messages. It seemed certain, then, that friends at home would have all anxiety removed, but there were mistakes in the official list first telegraphed. The experience of my own friends illustrates this: the Marconigram I wrote never got through to England; nor was my name ever mentioned in any list of the saved (even a week after landing in New York, I saw it in a black-edged 'final' list of the missing), and it seemed certain that I had never reached the *Carpathia*; so much so that, as I write, there are before me obituary notices from the English papers giving a short sketch of my life in England. After landing in New York and realising from the lists of the saved which a reporter showed me that my friends had no news since the *Titanic* sank on Monday morning until that night (Thursday 9 p.m.), I cabled to England at once (as I had but two shillings rescued from the *Titanic*, the White Star Line paid for the cables), but the messages were not delivered until 8.20 a.m. next morning. At 9 a.m. my friends read in the papers a short account of the disaster which I had supplied to the press, so that they knew of my safety and experiences in the wreck almost at the same time. I am grateful to remember that many of my friends in London refused to count me among the missing during the three days when I was so reported.

There is another side to this record of how the news came through, and a sad one, indeed. Again I wish it were not necessary to tell such things, but since they all bear on the equipment of the transatlantic lines – powerful Marconi apparatus, relays of operators, etc. – it is best they should be told. The name of an American gentleman – the same who sat near me in the library on Sunday afternoon and whom I identified later from a photograph – was consistently reported in the lists as saved and aboard the *Carpathia*: his son journeyed to New York to meet him, rejoicing at his deliverance, and never found him there. When I met his family some days later and was able to give them some details of his life aboard ship, it seemed almost cruel to tell them of the opposite experience that had befallen my friends at home.

Returning to the journey of the *Carpathia* – the last boatload of passengers was taken aboard at 8.30 a.m., the lifeboats were hauled on deck while the collapsibles were abandoned, and the *Carpathia* proceeded to steam round the scene of the wreck in the hope of picking up anyone floating on wreckage. Before doing so the captain arranged in the saloon a service over the spot where the *Titanic* sank, as nearly as could be calculated – a service, as he said, of respect to those who were lost and of gratitude for those who were saved.

She cruised round and round the scene, but found nothing to indicate there was any hope of picking up more passengers; and as the *Californian* had now arrived, followed shortly afterwards by the *Birma*, a Russian tramp steamer, Captain Rostron decided to leave any further search to them and to make all speed with the rescued to land. As we moved round, there was surprisingly little wreckage to be seen: wooden deckchairs and small pieces of other wood, but nothing of any size. But covering the sea in huge patches was a mass of reddish-yellow 'seaweed', as we called it for want of a name. It was said to be cork, but I never heard definitely its correct description.

The problem of where to land us had next to be decided. The *Carpathia* was bound for Gibraltar, and the captain might continue his journey there, landing us at the Azores on the way; but he would require more linen and provisions, the passengers were mostly women and children, ill-clad, dishevelled, and in need of many attentions he could not give them. Then, too, he would soon be out of the range of wireless communication, with the weak apparatus his ship had, and he soon decided against that course. Halifax was the nearest in point of distance, but this meant steaming north through the ice, and he thought his passengers did not want to see more ice. He headed back therefore to New York, which he had left the previous Thursday, working all afternoon along the edge of the icefield which stretched away north as far as the unaided eye could reach. I have wondered since if we could possibly have landed our passengers on this ice-floe from the lifeboats and gone back to pick up those swimming, had we known it was there; I should think it quite feasible to have done so. It was certainly an extraordinary sight to stand on deck and see the sea covered with solid ice, white and dazzling in the sun and dotted here and there with icebergs. We ran close up, only two or three hundred yards away, and steamed parallel to the floe, until it ended towards night and we saw to our infinite satisfaction the last of the icebergs and the field fading away astern. Many of the rescued have no wish ever to see an iceberg again. We learnt afterwards the field was nearly seventy miles long and twelve miles wide, and had lain between us and the *Birma* on her way to the rescue. Mr Boxhall testified that he had crossed the Grand Banks many times, but had never seen field ice before. The testimony of the captains and officers of other steamers in the neighbourhood is of the same kind: they had 'never seen so many icebergs this time of the year, or 'never seen such dangerous ice-floes and threatening bergs'. Undoubtedly the *Titanic* was faced that night with unusual and unexpected conditions of ice: the captain knew not the extent of these conditions, but he knew somewhat of their existence. Alas, that he heeded not their warning!

During the day, the bodies of eight of the crew were committed to the deep: four of them had been taken out of the boats dead and four died during the day. The engines were stopped and all passengers on deck bared their heads while a short service was read; when it was over the ship steamed on again to carry the living back to land.

The passengers on the *Carpathia* were by now hard at work finding clothing for the survivors: the barber's shop was raided for ties, collars, hairpins, combs, etc., of which it happened there was a large stock in hand; one good Samaritan went round the ship with a box of toothbrushes offering them indiscriminately to all. In some cases, clothing could not be found for the ladies and they spent the rest of the time on board in their dressing gowns and cloaks in which they came away from the *Titanic*. They even slept in them, for, in the absence of berths, women had to sleep on the floor of the saloons and in the library each night on straw *paillasses*, and here it was not possible to undress properly. The men were given the smoking room floor and a supply of blankets, but the room was small, and some elected to sleep out on deck. I found a pile of towels on the bathroom floor ready for next morning's baths, and made up a very comfortable bed on these. Later I was waked in the middle of the night by a man offering me a berth in his four-berth cabin: another occupant was unable to leave his berth for physical reasons, and so the cabin could not be given up to ladies.

On Tuesday the survivors met in the saloon and formed a committee among themselves to collect subscriptions for a general fund, out of which it was resolved by vote to provide as far as possible for the destitute among the steerage passengers, to present a loving cup to Captain Rostron and medals to the officers and crew of the *Carpathia*, and to divide any surplus among the crew of the *Titanic*. The work of this committee is not yet (1 June) at an end, but all the resolutions except the last one have been acted upon, and that is now receiving the attention of the committee. The presentations to the captain and crew were made the day the *Carpathia* returned to New York from her Mediterranean trip, and it is a pleasure to all the survivors to know that the United States Senate has recognised the service rendered to humanity by the *Carpathia* and has voted Captain Rostron a gold medal commemorative of the rescue. On the afternoon of Tuesday, I visited the steerage in company with a fellow passenger, to take down the names of all who were saved. We grouped them into nationalities – English, Irish, and Swedish mostly – and learnt from them their names and homes, the amount of money they possessed, and whether they had friends in America. The Irish girls almost universally had no money rescued from the wreck, and were going to friends in New York or places near, while the Swedish passengers, among whom were a considerable number of men, had saved the greater part of their money and in addition had railway tickets through to their destinations inland. The saving of their money marked a curious racial difference, for which I can offer no explanation: no doubt the Irish girls never had very much but they must have had the necessary amount fixed by the immigration laws. There were some pitiful cases of women with children and the husband lost; some with one or two children saved and the others lost; in one case, a whole family was missing, and only a friend left to tell of them. Among the Irish group was one girl of really remarkable beauty, black hair and deep violet eyes with long lashes, and perfectly shaped features, and quite young, not more than eighteen or twenty; I think she lost no relatives on the *Titanic*.

The following letter to the London *Times* is reproduced here to show something of what our feeling was on board the *Carpathia* towards the loss of the *Titanic*. It was written soon after we had the definite information on the Wednesday that ice warnings had been sent to the *Titanic*, and when we all felt that something must be done to awaken public opinion to safeguard ocean travel in the future. We were not aware, of course, how much the outside world knew, and it seemed well to do something to inform the English public of what had happened at as early an opportunity as possible. I have not had occasion to change any of the opinions expressed in this letter.

SIR

As one of few surviving Englishmen from the steamship *Titanic*, which sank in mid-Atlantic on Monday morning last, I am asking you to lay before your readers a few facts concerning the disaster, in the hope that something may be done in the near future to ensure the safety of that portion of the travelling public who use the Atlantic highway for business or pleasure.

I wish to dissociate myself entirely from any report that would seek to fix the responsibility on any person or persons or body of people, and by simply calling attention to matters of fact the authenticity of which is, I think, beyond question and can be established in any Court of Inquiry, to allow your readers to draw their own conclusions as to the responsibility for the collision.

First, that it was known to those in charge of the *Titanic* that we were in the iceberg region; that the atmospheric and temperature conditions suggested the near presence of icebergs; that a wireless message was received from a ship ahead of us warning us that they had been seen in the locality of which latitude and longitude were given.

Second, that at the time of the collision the *Titanic* was running at a high rate of speed.

Third, that the accommodation for saving passengers and crew was totally inadequate, being sufficient only for a total of about 950. This gave, with the highest possible complement of 3,400, a less than one in three chance of being saved in the case of accident.

Fourth, that the number landed in the *Carpathia*, approximately 700, is a high percentage of the possible 950, and bears excellent testimony to the courage, resource, and devotion to duty of the officers and crew of the vessel; many instances of their nobility and personal self-sacrifice are within our possession, and we know that they did all they could do with the means at their disposal.

Fifth, that the practice of running mail and passenger vessels through fog and iceberg regions at a high speed is a common one; they are timed to run almost as an express train is run, and they cannot, therefore, slow down more than a few knots in time of possible danger.

I have neither knowledge nor experience to say what remedies I consider should be applied; but, perhaps, the following suggestions may serve as a help:

First, that no vessel should be allowed to leave a British port without sufficient boat and other accommodation to allow each passenger and member of the crew a seat; and that at the time of booking this fact should be pointed out to a passenger, and the number of the seat in the particular boat allotted to him then.

Second, that as soon as is practicable after sailing each passenger should go through boat drill in company with the crew assigned to his boat.

Third, that each passenger boat engaged in the transatlantic service should be instructed to slow down to a few knots when in the iceberg region, and should be fitted with an efficient searchlight.

Yours faithfully,

LAWRENCE BEESLEY.

It seemed well, too, while on the *Carpathia* to prepare as accurate an account as possible of the disaster and to have this ready for the press, in order to calm public opinion and to forestall the incorrect and hysterical accounts which some American reporters are in the habit of preparing on occasions of this kind. The first impression is often the most permanent, and in a disaster of this magnitude, where exact and accurate information is so necessary, preparation of a report was essential. It was written in odd corners of the deck and saloon of the *Carpathia*, and fell, it seemed very happily, into the hands of the one reporter who could best deal with it, the Associated Press. I understand it was the first report that came through and had a good deal of the effect intended.

The *Carpathia* returned to New York in almost every kind of climatic conditions: icebergs, icefields and bitter cold to commence with; brilliant warm sun, thunder and lightning in the middle of one night (and so closely did the peal follow the flash that women in the saloon leaped up in alarm saying rockets were being sent up again); cold winds most of the time; fogs every morning and during a good part of one day, with the foghorn blowing constantly; rain; choppy sea with the spray blowing overboard and coming in through the saloon windows; we said we had almost everything but hot weather and stormy seas. So that when we were told that Nantucket Lightship had been sighted on Thursday morning from the bridge, a great sigh of relief went round to think New York and land would be reached before next morning.

There is no doubt that a good many felt the waiting period of those four days very trying: the ship crowded far beyond its limits of comfort, the want of necessities of clothing and toilet, and above all the anticipation of meeting with relatives on the pier, with, in many cases, the knowledge that other friends were left behind and would not return home again. A few looked forward to meeting on the pier their friends to whom they had said au revoir on the *Titanic*'s deck, brought there by a faster boat, they said, or at any rate to hear that they were following behind us in another boat: a very few, indeed, for the thought of the icy water and the many hours' immersion seemed to weigh against such a possibility; but we encouraged them to hope the *Californian* and the *Birma* had picked some up; stranger things have happened, and we had all been through strange experiences. But in the midst of this rather tense feeling, one fact stands out as remarkable – no one was ill. Captain Rostron testified that on Tuesday the doctor reported a clean bill of health, except for frostbites and shaken nerves. There were none of the illnesses supposed to follow from exposure for hours in the cold night – and, it must be remembered, a considerable number swam about for some time when the *Titanic* sank, and then either sat for hours in their wet things or lay flat on an upturned boat with the sea water washing partly over them until they were taken off in a lifeboat; no scenes of women weeping and brooding over their losses hour by hour until they were driven mad with grief – yet all this has been reported to the press by people on board the *Carpathia*. These women met their sorrow with the sublimest courage, came on deck and talked with their fellow men and women face to face, and in the midst of their loss did not forget to rejoice with those who had joined their friends on the *Carpathia*'s deck or come with them in a boat. There was no need for those ashore to call the *Carpathia* a 'death-ship', or to send coroners and coffins to the pier to meet her: her passengers were generally in good health and they did not pretend they were not.

Presently land came in sight, and very good it was to see it again: it was eight days since we left Southa..apton, but the time seemed to have 'stretched out to the crack of doom', and to have become eight weeks instead. So many dramatic incidents had been crowded into the last few days that the first four peaceful, uneventful days, marked by nothing that seared the memory, had faded almost out of recollection. It needed an effort to return to Southampton, Cherbourg and Queenstown, as though returning to some event of last year. I think we all realised that time may be measured more by events than by seconds and minutes: what the astronomer would call '2.20 a.m. 15 April 1912', the survivors called 'the sinking of the *Titanic*'; the 'hours' that followed were designated 'being adrift in an open sea', and '4.30 a.m.' was 'being rescued by the *Carpathia*'. The clock was a mental one, and the hours, minutes and seconds marked deeply on its face were emotions, strong and silent.

Surrounded by tugs of every kind, from which (as well as from every available building near the river) magnesium bombs were shot off by photographers, while reporters shouted for news of the disaster and photographs of passengers, the *Carpathia* drew slowly to her station at the Cunard pier, the gangways were pushed across, and we set foot at last on American soil, very thankful, grateful people.

The mental and physical condition of the rescued as they came ashore has, here again, been greatly exaggerated – one description says we were 'half-fainting, half-hysterical, bordering on hallucination, only now beginning to realise the horror'. It is unfortunate such pictures should be presented to the world. There were some painful scenes of meeting between relatives of those who were lost, but once again women showed their self-control and went through the ordeal in most cases with extraordinary calm. It is well to record that the same account added: 'A few, strangely enough, are calm and lucid'; if for 'few' we read 'a large majority', it will be much nearer the true description of the landing on the Cunard pier in New York. There seems to be no adequate reason why a report of such a scene should depict mainly the sorrow and grief, should seek for every detail to satisfy the horrible and the morbid in the human mind. The first questions the excited crowds of reporters asked as they crowded round were whether it was true that officers shot passengers, and then themselves; whether passengers shot each other; whether any scenes of horror had been noticed, and what they were.

It would have been well to have noticed the wonderful state of health of most of the rescued, their gratitude for their deliverance, the thousand and one things that gave cause for rejoicing. In the midst of so much description of the hysterical side of the scene, place should be found for the normal – and I venture to think the normal was the dominant feature in the landing that night. In the last chapter I shall try to record the persistence of the normal all through the disaster. Nothing has been a greater surprise than to find people that do not act in conditions of danger and grief as they would be generally supposed to act – and, I must add, as they are generally described as acting.

And so, with her work of rescue well done, the good ship *Carpathia* returned to New York. Everyone who came in her, everyone on the dock, and everyone who heard of her journey will agree with Captain Rostron when he says: 'I thank God that I was within wireless hailing distance, and that I got there in time to pick up the survivors of the wreck.'

8

The Lessons Taught by the Titanic's Loss

One of the most pitiful things in the relations of human beings to each other – the action and reaction of events that is called concretely 'human life' – is that every now and then some of them should be called upon to lay down their lives from no sense of imperative, calculated duty such as inspires the soldier or the sailor, but suddenly, without any previous knowledge or warning of danger, without any opportunity of escape, and without any desire to risk such conditions of danger of their own free will. It is a blot on our civilisation that these things are necessary from time to time, to arouse those responsible for the safety of human life from the lethargic selfishness which has governed them. The Titanic's two thousand odd passengers went aboard thinking they were on an absolutely safe ship, and all the time there were many people – designers, builders, experts, government officials – who knew there were insufficient boats on board, that the Titanic had no right to go fast in iceberg regions – who knew these things and took no steps and enacted no laws to prevent their happening. Not that they omitted to do these things deliberately, but were lulled into a state of selfish inaction from which it needed such a tragedy as this to arouse them. It was a cruel necessity which demanded that a few should die to arouse many millions to a sense of their own insecurity, to the fact that for years the possibility of such a disaster has been imminent. Passengers have known none of these things, and while no good end would have been served by relating to them needless tales of danger on the high seas, one thing is certain – that, had they known them, many would not have travelled in such conditions and thereby safeguards would soon have been forced on the builders, the companies, and the Government. But there were people who knew and did not fail to call attention to the dangers: in the House of Commons the matter has been frequently brought up privately, and an American naval officer, Captain E. K. Roden, in an article that has since been widely reproduced, called attention to the defects of this very ship, the *Titanic* – taking her as an example of all other liners – and pointed out that she was not unsinkable and had not proper boat accommodation.

The question, then, of responsibility for the loss of the *Titanic* must be considered: not from any idea that blame should be laid here or there and a scapegoat provided – that is a waste of time. But if a fixing of responsibility leads to quick and efficient remedy, then it should be done relentlessly: our simple duty to those whom the *Titanic* carried down with her demands no less. Dealing first with the precautions for the safety of the ship as apart from safety appliances, there can be no question, I suppose, that the direct responsibility for the loss of the *Titanic* and so many lives must be laid on her captain. He was responsible for setting the course, day by day and hour by hour, for the speed she was travelling; and he alone would have the power to decide whether or not speed must be slackened with icebergs ahead. No officer would have any right to interfere in the navigation, although they would no doubt be consulted. Nor would any official connected with the management of the line – Mr Ismay, for example – be allowed to direct the captain in these matters, and there is no evidence that he ever tried to do so. The very fact that the captain of a ship has such absolute authority increases his responsibility enormously. Even supposing the White Star Line and Mr Ismay had urged him before sailing to make a record – again an assumption – they cannot be held directly responsible for the collision: he was in charge of the lives of everyone on board and no one but he was supposed to estimate the risk of travelling at the speed he did, when ice was reported ahead of him. His action cannot be justified on the ground of prudent seamanship.

But the question of indirect responsibility raises at once many issues and, I think, removes from Captain Smith a good deal of personal responsibility for the loss of his ship. Some of these issues it will be well to consider.

In the first place, disabusing our minds again of the knowledge that the *Titanic* struck an iceberg and sank, let us estimate the probabilities of such a thing happening. An iceberg is small and occupies little room by comparison with the broad ocean on which it floats; and the chances of another small object like a ship colliding with it and being sunk are very small: the chances are, as a matter of fact, one in a million. This is not a figure of speech: that is the actual risk for total loss by collision with an iceberg as accepted by insurance companies. The one-in-a-million accident was what sunk the *Titanic*.

Even so, had Captain Smith been alone in taking that risk, he would have had to bear all the blame for the resulting disaster. But it seems he is not alone: the same risk has been taken over and over again by fast mail-passenger liners, in fog and in iceberg regions. Their captains have taken the long – very long – chance many times and won every time; he took it as he had done many times before, and lost. Of course, the chances that night of striking an iceberg were much greater than one in a million: they had been enormously increased by the extreme southerly position of icebergs and field ice and by the unusual number of the former. Thinking over the scene that met our eyes from the deck of the *Carpathia* after we boarded her – the great number of icebergs wherever the eye could reach – the chances of *not* hitting one in the darkness of the night seemed small. Indeed, the more one thinks about the *Carpathia* coming at full speed through all those icebergs in the darkness, the more inexplicable does it seem. True, the captain had an extra lookout watch and every sense of every man on the bridge alert to detect the least sign of danger, and again he was not going so fast as the *Titanic* and would have his ship under more control; but granted all that, he appears to have taken a great risk as he dogged and twisted round the awful 200-foot monsters in the dark night. Does it mean that the risk is not so great as we who have seen the abnormal and not the normal side of taking risks with icebergs might suppose? He had his own ship and passengers to consider, and he had no right to take too great a risk.

But Captain Smith could not know icebergs were there in such numbers: what warnings he had of them is not yet thoroughly established – there were probably three – but it is in the highest degree unlikely that he knew that any vessel had seen them in such quantities as we saw them Monday morning; in fact, it is unthinkable. He thought, no doubt, he was taking an ordinary risk, and it turned out to be an extraordinary one. To read some criticisms it would seem as if he deliberately ran his ship in defiance of all custom through a region infested with icebergs, and did a thing which no one has ever done before; that he outraged all precedent by not slowing down. But it is plain that he did not. Every captain who has run full speed through fog and iceberg regions is to blame for the disaster as much as he is:

they got through and he did not. Other liners can go faster than the *Titanic* could possibly do; had they struck ice they would have been injured even more deeply than she was, for it must not be forgotten that the force of impact varies as the *square* of the velocity – i.e., it is four times as much at sixteen knots as at eight knots, nine times as much at twenty-four, and so on. And with not much margin of time left for these fast boats, they must go full speed ahead nearly all the time. Remember how they advertise to 'Leave New York Wednesday, dine in London the following Monday', – and it is done regularly, much as an express train is run to time. Their officers, too, would have been less able to avoid a collision than Murdock of the *Titanic* was, for at the greater speed, they would be on the iceberg in shorter time. Many passengers can tell of crossing with fog a good deal of the way, sometimes almost all the way, and they have been only a few hours late at the end of the journey.

So that it is the custom that is at fault, not one particular captain. Custom is established largely by demand, and supply too is the answer to demand. What the public demanded the White Star Line supplied, and so both the public and the line are concerned with the question of indirect responsibility.

The public has demanded, more and more every year, greater speed as well as greater comfort, and by ceasing to patronise the low-speed boats has gradually forced the pace to what it is at present. Not that speed in itself is a dangerous thing – it is sometimes much safer to go quickly than slowly – but that, given the facilities for speed and the stimulus exerted by the constant public demand for it, occasions arise when the judgement of those in command of a ship becomes swayed – largely unconsciously, no doubt – in favour of taking risks which the smaller liners would never take. The demand on the skipper of a boat like the *Californian*, for example, which lay hove-to nineteen miles away with her engines stopped, is infinitesimal compared with that on Captain Smith. An old traveller told me on the *Carpathia* that he has often grumbled to the officers for what he called absurd precautions in lying-to and wasting his time, which he regarded as very valuable; but after hearing of the *Titanic*'s loss he recognised that he was to some extent responsible for the speed at which she had travelled, and would never be so again. He had been one of the travelling public who had constantly demanded to be taken to his journey's end in the shortest possible time, and had 'made a row' about it if he was likely to be late. There are some businessmen to whom the five or six days on board are exceedingly irksome and represent a waste of time; even an hour saved at the journey's end is a consideration to them. And if the demand is not always a conscious one, it is there as an unconscious factor always urging the highest speed of which the ship is capable. The man who demands fast travel unreasonably must undoubtedly take his share in the responsibility. He asks to be taken over at a speed which will land him in something over four days; he forgets perhaps that Columbus took ninety days in a forty-ton boat, and that only fifty years ago paddle steamers took six weeks, and all the time the demand is greater and the strain is more: the public demand speed and luxury; the lines supply it, until presently the safety limit is reached, the undue risk is taken – and the *Titanic* goes down. All of us who have cried for greater speed must take our share in the responsibility. The expression of such a desire and the discontent with so-called slow travel are the seed sown in the minds of men, to bear fruit presently in an insistence on greater speed. We may not have done so directly, but we may perhaps have talked about it and thought about it, and we know no action begins without thought.

The White Star Line has received very rough handling from some of the press, but the greater part of this criticism seems to be unwarranted and to arise from the desire to find a scapegoat. After all they had made better provision for the passengers the *Titanic* carried than any other line has done, for they had built what they believed to be a huge lifeboat, unsinkable in all ordinary conditions. Those who embarked in her were almost certainly in the safest ship (along with the *Olympic*) afloat: she was probably quite immune from the ordinary effects of wind, waves and collisions at sea, and needed to fear nothing but running on a rock or, what was worse, a floating iceberg; for the effects of collision were, so far as damage was concerned, the same as if it had been a rock, and the danger greater, for one is charted and the other is not. Then, too, while the theory of the unsinkable boat has been destroyed at the same time as the boat itself, we should not forget that it served a useful purpose on deck that night – it eliminated largely the possibility of panic, and those rushes for the boats which might have swamped some of them. I do not wish for a moment to suggest that such things would have happened, because the more information that comes to hand of the conduct of the people on board, the more wonderful seems the complete self-control of all, even when the last boats had gone and nothing but the rising waters met their eyes – only that the generally entertained theory rendered such things less probable. The theory, indeed, was really a safeguard, though built on a false premise.

There is no evidence that the White Star Line instructed the captain to push the boat or to make any records: the probabilities are that no such attempt would be made on the first trip. The general instructions to their commanders bear quite the other interpretation: it will be well to quote them in full as issued to the press during the sittings of the United States Senate Committee:

Instructions to Commanders

Commanders must distinctly understand that the issue of regulations does not in any way relieve them from responsibility for the safe and efficient navigation of their respective vessels, and they are also enjoined to remember that they must run no risks which might by any possibility result in accident to their ships. It is to be hoped that they will ever bear in mind that the safety of the lives and property entrusted to their care is the ruling principle that should govern them in the navigation of their vessels, and that no supposed gain in expedition or saving of time on the voyage is to be purchased at the risk of accident.

Commanders are reminded that the steamers are to a great extent uninsured, and that their own livelihood, as well as the company's success, depends upon immunity from accident; no precaution which ensures safe navigation is to be considered excessive.

Nothing could be plainer than these instructions, and had they been obeyed, the disaster would never have happened: they warn commanders against the only thing left as a menace to their unsinkable boat – the lack of 'precaution which ensures safe navigation'.

In addition, the White Star Line had complied to the full extent with the requirements of the British Government: their ship had been subjected to an inspection so rigid that, as one officer remarked in evidence, it became a nuisance. The Board of Trade employs the best experts, and knows the dangers that attend ocean travel and the precautions that should be taken by every commander. If these precautions are not taken, it will be necessary to legislate until they are. No motorist is allowed to career at full speed along a public highway in dangerous conditions, and it should be an offence for a captain to do the same on the high seas with a ship full of unsuspecting passengers. They have entrusted their lives to the government of their country – through its regulations – and they are entitled to the same protection in mid-Atlantic as they are in Oxford Street or Broadway. The open sea should no longer be regarded as a neutral zone where no country's police laws are operative.

Of course there are difficulties in the way of drafting international regulations: many governments would have to be consulted and many difficulties that seem insuperable overcome; but that is the purpose for which governments are employed, that is why experts and ministers of governments are appointed and paid – to overcome difficulties for the people who appoint them and who expect them, among other things, to protect their lives.

The American Government must share the same responsibility: it is useless to attempt to fix it on the British Board of Trade for the reason that the boats were built in England and inspected there by British officials. They carried American citizens largely, and entered American ports. It would have been the simplest matter for the United States Government to veto the entry of any ship which did not conform to its laws of regulating speed in conditions of fog and icebergs – had they provided such laws. The fact is that the American nation has practically no mercantile marine, and in time of a disaster such as this it forgets, perhaps, that it has exactly the same right – and therefore the same responsibility – as the British Government to inspect, and to legislate: the right that is easily enforced by refusal to allow entry. The regulation of speed in dangerous regions could well be undertaken by some fleet of international police patrol vessels, with power to stop if necessary any boat found guilty of reckless racing. The additional duty of warning ships of the exact locality of icebergs could be performed by these boats. It would not of course be possible or advisable to fix a 'speed limit', because the region of icebergs varies in position as the icebergs float south, varies in point of danger as they melt and disappear, and the whole question has to be left largely to the judgement of the captain on the spot; but it would be possible to make it an offence against the law to go beyond a certain speed in known conditions of danger.

So much for the question of regulating speed on the high seas. The secondary question of safety appliances is governed by the same principle – that, in the last analysis, it is not the captain, not the passenger, not the builders and owners, but the governments through their experts, who are to be held responsible for the provision of lifesaving devices. Morally, of course, the owners and builders are responsible, but at present moral responsibility is too weak an incentive in human affairs – that is the miserable part of the whole wretched business – to induce owners generally to make every possible provision for the lives of those in their charge; to place human safety so far above every other consideration that no plan shall be left unconsidered, no device left untested, by which passengers can escape from a sinking ship. But it is not correct to say, as has been said frequently, that it is greed and dividend-hunting that have characterised the policy of the steamship companies in their failure to provide safety appliances: these things in themselves are not expensive. They have vied with each other in making their lines attractive in point of speed, size and comfort, and they have been quite justified in doing so: such things are the product of ordinary competition between commercial houses.

Where they have all failed morally is to extend to their passengers the consideration that places their lives as of more interest to them than any other conceivable thing. They are not alone in this: thousands of other people have done the same thing and would do it today – in factories, in workshops, in mines, did not the government intervene and insist on safety precautions. The thing is a defect in human life of today

– thoughtlessness for the well-being of our fellow men; and we are all guilty of it in some degree. It is folly for the public to rise up now and condemn the steamship companies: their failing is the common failing of the immorality of indifference.

The remedy is the law, and it is the only remedy at present that will really accomplish anything. The British law on the subject dates from 1894, and requires only twenty boats for a ship the size of the *Titanic*: the owners and builders have obeyed this law and fulfilled their legal responsibility. Increase this responsibility and they will fulfil it again – and the matter is ended so far as appliances are concerned. It should perhaps be mentioned that in a period of ten years only nine passengers were lost on British ships: the law seemed to be sufficient in fact.

The position of the American Government, however, is worse than that of the British Government. Its regulations require more than double the boat accommodation which the British regulations do, and yet it has allowed hundreds of thousands of its subjects to enter its ports on boats that defied its own laws. Had their government not been guilty of the same indifference, passengers would not have been allowed aboard any British ship lacking in boat accommodation – the simple expedient again of refusing entry. The reply of the British Government to the Senate Committee, accusing the Board of Trade of 'insufficient requirements and lax inspection', might well be – 'Ye have a law: see to it yourselves!'

It will be well now to consider briefly the various appliances that have been suggested to ensure the safety of passengers and crew, and in doing so it may be remembered that the average man and woman has the same right as the expert to consider and discuss these things: they are not so technical as to prevent anyone of ordinary intelligence from understanding their construction. Using the term in its widest sense, we come first to:

Bulkheads & Watertight Compartments

It is impossible to attempt a discussion here of the exact constructional details of these parts of a ship; but in order to illustrate briefly what is the purpose of having bulkheads, we may take the *Titanic* as an example. She was divided into sixteen compartments by fifteen transverse steel walls called bulkheads. If a hole is made in the side of the ship in any one compartment, steel watertight doors seal off the only openings in that compartment and separate it as a damaged unit from the rest of the ship and the vessel is brought to land in safety. Ships have even put into the nearest port for inspection after collision, and finding only one compartment full of water and no other damage, have left again, for their home port without troubling to disembark passengers and effect repairs.

The design of the *Titanic's* bulkheads calls for some attention. The *Scientific American*, in an excellent article on the comparative safety of the *Titanic's* and other types of watertight compartments, draws attention to the following weaknesses in the former – from the point of view of possible collision with an iceberg. She had no longitudinal bulkheads, which would subdivide her into smaller compartments and prevent the water filling the whole of a large compartment. Probably, too, the length of a large compartment was in any case too great – fifty-three feet.

The *Mauretania*, on the other hand, in addition to transverse bulkheads, is fitted with longitudinal torpedo bulkheads, and the space between them and the side of the ship is utilised as a coal bunker. Then, too, in the *Mauretania* all bulkheads are carried up to the top deck, whereas in the case of the *Titanic* they reached in some parts only to the saloon deck and in others to a lower deck still – the weakness of this being that, when the water reached to the top of a bulkhead as the ship sank by the head, it flowed over and filled the next compartment. The British Admiralty, which subsidises the *Mauretania* and *Lusitania* as fast cruisers in time of war, insisted on this type of construction, and it is considered vastly better than that used in the *Titanic*. The writer of the article thinks it possible that these ships might not have sunk as the result of a similar collision. But the ideal ship from the point of bulkhead construction, he considers to have been the *Great Eastern*, constructed many years ago by the famous engineer Brunel. So thorough was her system of compartments divided and subdivided by many transverse and longitudinal bulkheads that when she tore a hole eighty feet long in her side by striking a rock, she reached port in safety. Unfortunately the weight and cost of this method was so great that his plan was subsequently abandoned.

But it would not be just to say that the construction of the *Titanic* was a serious mistake on the part of the White Star Line or her builders, on the ground that her bulkheads were not so well constructed as those of the *Lusitania* and *Mauretania*, which were built to fulfil British Admiralty regulations for time of war – an extraordinary risk which no builder of a passenger steamer – as such – would be expected to take into consideration when designing the vessel. It should be constantly borne in mind that the *Titanic* met extraordinary conditions on the night of the collision: she was probably the safest ship afloat in all ordinary conditions. Collision with an iceberg is not an ordinary risk; but this disaster will probably result in altering the whole construction of bulkheads and compartments to the *Great Eastern* type, in order to include the one-in-a-million risk of iceberg collision and loss.

Here comes in the question of increased cost of construction, and in addition the great loss of cargo-carrying space with decreased earning capacity, both of which will mean an increase in the passenger rates. This the travelling public will have to face and undoubtedly will be willing to face for the satisfaction of knowing that what was so confidently affirmed by passengers on the *Titanic*'s deck that night of the collision will then be really true – that 'we are on an unsinkable boat' – so far as human forethought can devise. After all, this *must* be the solution to the problem how best to ensure safety at sea. Other safety appliances are useful and necessary, but not useable in certain conditions of weather. The ship itself must always be the 'safety appliance' that is really trustworthy, and nothing must be left undone to ensure this.

Wireless Apparatus & Operators

The range of the apparatus might well be extended, but the principal defect is the lack of an operator for night duty on some ships. The awful fact that the *Californian* lay a few miles away, able to save every soul on board, and could not catch the message because the operator was asleep, seems too cruel to dwell upon. Even on the *Carpathia*, the operator was on the point of retiring when the message arrived, and we should have been much longer afloat – and some boats possibly swamped – had he not caught the message when he did. It has been suggested that officers should have a working knowledge of wireless telegraphy, and this is no doubt a wise provision. It would enable them to supervise the work of the operators more closely and from all the evidence, this seems a necessity. The exchange of vitally important messages between a sinking ship and those rushing to her rescue should be under the control of an experienced officer. To take but one example – Bride testified that after giving the *Birma* the 'CQD' message and the position (incidentally Signer Marconi has stated that this has been abandoned in favour of 'SOS') and getting a reply, they got into touch with the *Carpathia*, and while talking with her were interrupted by the *Birma* asking what was the matter. No doubt it was the duty of the *Birma* to come at once without asking any questions, but the reply from the *Titanic*, telling the *Birma*'s operator not to be a 'fool' by interrupting, seems to have been a needless waste of precious moments: to reply 'We are sinking' would have taken no longer, especially when in their own estimation of the strength of the signals they thought the *Birma* was the nearer ship. It is well to notice that some large liners have already a staff of three operators.

Submarine Signalling Apparatus
There are occasions when wireless apparatus is useless as a means of saving life at sea promptly.

One of its weaknesses is that when the ships' engines are stopped, messages can no longer be sent out, that is, with the system at present adopted. It will be remembered that the *Titanic*'s messages got gradually fainter and then ceased altogether as she came to rest with her engines shut down.

Again, in fogs – and most accidents occur in fogs – while wireless informs of the accident, it does not enable one ship to locate another closely enough to take off her passengers at once. There is as yet no method known by which wireless telegraphy will fix the direction of a message; and after a ship has been in fog for any considerable length of time it is more difficult to give the exact position to another vessel bringing help.

Nothing could illustrate these two points better than the story of how the *Baltic* found the *Republic* in the year 1909, in a dense fog off Nantucket Lightship, when the latter was drifting helplessly after collision with the *Florida*. The *Baltic* received a wireless message stating the *Republic*'s condition and the information that she was in touch with Nantucket through a submarine bell which she could hear ringing. The *Baltic* turned and went towards the position in the fog, picked up the submarine bell signal from Nantucket, and then began searching near this position for the *Republic*. It took her twelve hours to find the damaged ship, zigzagging across a circle within which she thought the *Republic* might lie. In a rough sea it is doubtful whether the *Republic* would have remained afloat long enough for the *Baltic* to find her and take off all her passengers.

Now on these two occasions when wireless telegraphy was found to be unreliable, the usefulness of the submarine bell at once becomes apparent. The *Baltic* could have gone unerringly to the *Republic* in the dense fog had the latter been fitted with a submarine emergency bell. It will perhaps be well to spend a little time describing the submarine signalling apparatus to see how this result could have been obtained: twelve anxious hours in a dense fog on a ship which was injured so badly that she subsequently foundered, is an experience which every appliance known to human invention should be enlisted to prevent.

Submarine signalling has never received that public notice which wireless telegraphy has, for the reason that it does not appeal so readily to the popular mind. That it is an absolute necessity to every ship carrying passengers – or carrying anything, for that matter – is beyond question. It is an additional safeguard that no ship can afford to be without.

There are many occasions when the atmosphere fails lamentably as a medium for carrying messages. When fog falls down, as it does sometimes in a moment, on the hundreds of ships coasting down the traffic ways round our shores – ways which are defined so easily in clear weather and with such difficulty in fogs – the hundreds of lighthouses and lightships which serve as warning beacons, and on which many millions of money have been spent, are for all practical purposes as useless to the navigator as if they had never been built: he is just as helpless as if he were back in the years before 1514, when Trinity House was granted a charter by Henry VIII 'for the relief ... of the shipping of this realm of England', and began a system of lights on the shores, of which the present chain of lighthouses and lightships is the outcome.

Nor is the foghorn much better: the presence of different layers of fog and air, and their varying densities, which cause both reflection and refraction of sound, prevent the air from being a reliable medium for carrying it. Now, submarine signalling has none of these defects, for the medium is water, subject to no such variable conditions as the air. Its density is practically non-variable, and sound travels through it at the rate of 4,400 feet per second, without deviation or reflection.

The apparatus consists of a bell designed to ring either pneumatically from a lightship, electrically from the shore (the bell itself being a tripod at the bottom of the sea), automatically from a floating bell-buoy, or by hand from a ship or boat. The sound travels from the bell in every direction, like waves in a pond, and falls, it may be, on the side of a ship. The receiving apparatus is fixed inside the skin of the ship and consists of a small iron tank, 16 inches square and 18 inches deep. The front of the tank facing the ship's iron skin is missing and the tank, being filled with water, is bolted to the framework and sealed firmly to the ship's side by rubber facing. In this way a portion of the ship's iron hull is washed by the sea on one side and water in the tank on the other. Vibrations from a bell ringing at a distance fall on the iron side, travel through, and strike on two microphones hanging in the tank. These microphones transmit the sound along wires to the chart room, where telephones convey the message to the officer on duty.

There are two of these tanks or 'receivers' fitted against the ship's side, one on the port and one on the starboard side, near the bows, and as far down below the water level as is possible. The direction of sounds coming to the microphones hanging in these tanks can be estimated by switching alternately to the port and starboard tanks. If the sound is of greater intensity on the port side, then the bell signalling is off the port bows; and similarly on the starboard side.

The ship is turned towards the sound until the same volume of sound is heard from both receivers, when the bell is known to be dead ahead. So accurate is this in practice that a trained operator can steer his ship in the densest fog directly to a lightship or any other point where a submarine bell is sending its warning beneath the sea. It must be repeated that the medium in which these signals are transmitted is a constant one, not subject to any of the limitations and variations imposed on the atmosphere and the ether as media for the transmission of light, blasts of a foghorn, and wireless vibrations. At present the chief use of submarine signalling is from the shore or a lightship to ships at sea, and not from ship to ship or from ship to the shore: in other words ships carry only receiving apparatus, and lighthouses and lightships use only signalling apparatus. Some of the lighthouses and lightships on our coasts already have these submarine bells in addition to their lights, and in bad weather the bells send out their messages to warn ships of their proximity to a danger point. This invention enables ships to pick up the sound of bell after bell on a coast and run along it in the densest fog almost as well as in daylight; passenger steamers coming into port do not have to wander about in the fog, groping their way blindly into harbour. By having a code of rings, and judging by the intensity of the sound, it is possible to tell almost exactly where a ship is in relation to the coast or to some lightship. The British Admiralty report in 1906 said: 'If the lightships round the coast were fitted with submarine bells, it would be possible for ships fitted with receiving apparatus to navigate in fog with almost as great certainty as in clear weather.' And the following remark of a

captain engaged in coast service is instructive. H
cut down expenses by omitting the submarine s⌣
but replied: 'I would rather take out the wireless. That ⌣
me to tell other people where I am. The submarine signal ena⌣
me to find out where I am myself.'

The range of the apparatus is not so wide as that of wireless telegraphy, varying from 10 to 15 miles for a large ship (although instances of 20 to 30 are on record), and from 3 to 8 miles for a small ship.

At present the receiving apparatus is fixed on only some 650 steamers of the merchant marine, these being mostly the first class passenger liners. There is no question that it should be installed, along with wireless apparatus, on every ship of over 1,000 tons gross tonnage. Equally important is the provision of signalling apparatus on board ships: it is obviously just as necessary to transmit a signal as to receive one; but at present the sending of signals from ships has not been perfected. The invention of signal-transmitting apparatus to be used while the ship is under way is as yet in the experimental stage; but while she is at rest a bell similar to those used by lighthouses can be sunk over her side and rung by hand with exactly the same effect. But liners are not provided with them (they cost only £60!). As mentioned before, with another £60 spent on the *Republic*'s equipment, the *Baltic* could have picked up her bell and steered direct to her – just as they both heard the bell of Nantucket Lightship. Again, if the *Titanic* had been provided with a bell and the *Californian* with receiving apparatus – neither of them was – the officer on the bridge could have heard the signals from the telephones near.

A smaller size for use in lifeboats is provided, and would be heard by receiving apparatus for approximately five miles. If we had hung one of these bells over the side of the lifeboats afloat that night we should ave been free from the anxiety of being run down as we lay across the *Carpathia*'s path, without a light. Or if we had gone adrift in a dense fog and wandered miles apart from each other on the sea (as we inevitably should have done), the *Carpathia* could still have picked up each boat individually by means of the bell signal.

In those ships fitted with receiving apparatus, at least one officer is obliged to understand the working of the apparatus: a very wise precaution, and, as suggested above, one that should be taken with respect to wireless apparatus also.

It was a very great pleasure to me to see all this apparatus in manufacture and in use at one of the principal submarine signalling works in America and to hear some of the remarkable stories of its value in actual practice. I was struck by the aptness of the motto adopted by them – 'De profundis clamavi' – in relation to the *Titanic*'s end and the calls of our passengers from the sea when she sank. 'Out of the deep have I called unto Thee' is indeed a suitable motto for those who are doing all they can to prevent such calls arising from their fellow men and women 'out of the deep'.

Fixing of Steamship Routes

The 'lanes' along which the liners travel are fixed by agreement among the steamship companies in consultation with the Hydrographic departments of the different countries. These routes are arranged so that east-bound steamers are always a number of miles away from those going west, and thus the danger of collision between east- and west-bound vessels is entirely eliminated. The 'lanes' can be moved farther south if icebergs threaten, and north again when the danger is removed. Of course the farther south they are placed, the longer the journey to be made, and the longer the time spent on board, with consequent grumbling by some passengers. For example, the lanes since the disaster to the *Titanic* have been moved one hundred miles farther south, which means one hundred and eighty miles longer journey, taking eight hours.

The only real precaution against colliding with icebergs is to go south of the place where they are likely to be: there is no other way.

Lifeboats

The provision was of course woefully inadequate. The only humane plan is to have a numbered seat in a boat assigned to each passenger and member of the crew. It would seem well to have this number pointed out at the time of booking a berth, and to have a plan in each cabin showing where the boat is and how to get to it the most direct way – a most important consideration with a ship like the *Titanic* with over two miles of deck space. Boat drills of the passengers and crew of each boat should be held, under compulsion, as soon as possible after leaving port. I asked an officer as to the possibility of having such a drill immediately after the gangways are withdrawn and before the tugs are allowed to haul the ship out of dock, but he says the difficulties are almost insuperable at such a time. If so, the drill should be conducted in sections as soon as possible after sailing, and should be conducted in a thorough manner. Children in school are called upon suddenly to go through fire drill, and there is no reason why passengers on board ship should not be similarly trained. So much depends on order and readiness in time of danger. Undoubtedly, the whole subject of manning, provisioning, loading and lowering of lifeboats should be in the hands of an expert officer, who should have no other duties. The modern liner has become far too big to permit the captain to exercise control over the whole ship, and all vitally important subdivisions should be controlled by a separate authority. It seems a piece of bitter irony to remember that on the *Titanic* a special chef was engaged at a large salary – larger perhaps than that of any officer – and no boatmaster (or some such officer) was considered necessary. The general system again – not criminal neglect, as some hasty criticisms would say, but lack of consideration for our fellow man, the placing of luxurious attractions above that kindly forethought that allows no precaution to be neglected for even the humblest passenger. But it must not be overlooked that the provision of sufficient lifeboats on deck is not evidence they will all be launched easily or all the passengers taken off safely. It must be remembered that ideal conditions prevailed that night for launching boats from the decks of the *Titanic*: there was no list that prevented the boats getting away, they could be launched on both sides, and when they were lowered the sea was so calm that they pulled away without any of the smashing against the side that is possible in rough seas. Sometimes it would mean that only those boats on the side sheltered from a heavy sea could ever get away, and this would at once halve the boat accommodation. And when launched, there would be the danger of swamping in such a heavy sea. All things considered, lifeboats might be the poorest sort of safeguard in certain conditions.

Liferafts are said to be much inferior to lifeboats in a rough sea, and collapsible boats made of canvas and thin wood soon decay under exposure to weather and are danger-traps at a critical moment.

Some of the lifeboats should be provided with motors, to keep the boats together and to tow if necessary. The launching is an important matter: the *Titanic's* davits worked excellently and no doubt were largely responsible for all the boats getting away safely: they were far superior to those on most liners.

Pontoons

After the sinking of the *Bourgogne*, when two Americans lost their lives, a prize of £4,000 was offered by their heirs for the best lifesaving device applicable to ships at sea. A board sat to consider the various appliances sent in by competitors, and finally awarded the prize to an Englishman, whose design provided for a flat structure the width of the ship, which could be floated off when required and would accommodate several hundred passengers. It has never been adopted by any steamship line. Other similar designs are known, by which the whole of the after deck can be pushed over from the stern by a ratchet arrangement, with air-tanks below to buoy it up: it seems to be a practical suggestion.

One point where the *Titanic* management failed lamentably was to provide a properly trained crew to each lifeboat. The rowing was in most cases execrable. There is no more reason why a steward should be able to row than a passenger – less so than some of the passengers who were lost; men of leisure accustomed to all kinds of sport (including rowing), and in addition probably more fit physically than a steward to row for hours on the open sea. And if a steward cannot row, he has no right to be at an oar; so that, under the unwritten rule that passengers take precedence of the crew when there is not sufficient accommodation for all (a situation that should never be allowed to arise again, for a member of the crew should have an equal opportunity with a passenger to save his life), the majority of stewards and cooks should have stayed behind and passengers have come instead: they could not have been of less use, and they might have been of more. It will be remembered that the proportion of crew saved to passengers was 210 to 495, a high proportion.

Another point arises out of these figures – deduct 21 members of the crew who were stewardesses, and 189 men of the crew are left as against the 495 passengers. Of these some got on the overturned collapsible boat after the *Titanic* sank, and a few were picked up by the lifeboats, but these were not many in all. Now with the 17 boats brought to the *Carpathia* and an average of six of the crew to man each boat – probably a higher average than was realised – we get a total of 102 who should have been saved as against 189 who actually were. There were, as is known, stokers and stewards in the boats who were not members of the lifeboats' crews. It may seem heartless to analyse figures in this way, and suggest that some of the crew who got to the *Carpathia* never should have done so; but, after all, passengers took their passage under certain rules – written and unwritten – and one is that in times of danger the servants of the company in whose boats they sail shall first of all see to the safety of the passengers before thinking of their own. There were only 126 men passengers saved as against 189 of the crew, and 661 men lost as against 686 of the crew, so that actually the crew had a greater percentage saved than the men passengers – 22 per cent against 16.

But steamship companies are faced with real difficulties in this matter. The crews are never the same for two voyages together: they sign on for the one trip, then perhaps take a berth on shore as waiters, stokers in hotel furnace rooms, etc. – to resume life on board any other ship that is handy when the desire comes to go to sea again. They can in no sense be regarded as part of a homogeneous crew, subject to regular discipline and educated to appreciate the morale of a particular liner, as a man of war's crew is.

Searchlights

These seem an absolute necessity, and the wonder is that they have not been fitted before to all ocean liners. Not only are they of use in lighting up the sea a long distance ahead, but as flashlight signals they permit of communication with other ships. As I write, through the window can be seen the flashes from river steamers plying up the Hudson in New York, each with its searchlight, examining the river, lighting up the bank for hundreds of yards ahead, and bringing every object within its reach into prominence. They are regularly used too in the Suez Canal.

I suppose there is no question that the collision would have been avoided had a searchlight been fitted to the *Titanic's* masthead: the climatic conditions for its use must have been ideal that night. There are other things besides icebergs: derelicts are reported from time to time, and fishermen lie in the lanes without lights. They would not always be of practical use, however. They would be of no service in heavy rain, in fog, in snow, or in flying spray, and the effect is sometimes to dazzle the eyes of the lookout.

While writing of the lookout, much has been made of the omission to provide the lookout on the *Titanic* with glasses. The general opinion of officers seems to be that it is better not to provide them, but to rely on good eyesight and wide-awake men. After all, in a question of actual practice, the opinion of officers should be accepted as final, even if it seems to the landsman the better thing to provide glasses.

Cruising Lightships

One or two internationally owned and controlled lightships, fitted with every known device for signalling and communication, would rob those regions of most of their terrors. They could watch and chart the icebergs, report their exact position, the amount and direction of daily drift in the changing currents that are found there. To them, too, might be entrusted the duty of police patrol.

9

Some Impressions

No one can pass through an event like the wreck of the *Titanic* without recording mentally many impressions, deep and vivid, of what has been seen and felt. In so far as such impressions are of benefit to mankind they should not be allowed to pass unnoticed, and this chapter is an attempt to picture how people thought and felt from the time they first heard of the disaster to the landing in New York, when there was opportunity to judge of events somewhat from a distance. While it is to some extent a personal record, the mental impressions of other survivors have been compared and found to be in many cases closely in agreement. Naturally it is very imperfect, and pretends to be no more than a sketch of the way people act under the influence of strong emotions produced by imminent danger.

In the first place, the principal fact that stands out is the almost entire absence of any expressions of fear or alarm on the part of passengers, and the conformity to the normal on the part of almost everyone. I think it is no exaggeration to say that those who read of the disaster quietly at home, and pictured to themselves the scene as the *Titanic* was sinking, had more of the sense of horror than those who stood on the deck and watched her go down inch by inch. The fact is that the sense of fear came to the passengers very slowly – a result of the absence of any signs of danger and the peaceful night – and as it became evident gradually that there was serious damage to the ship, the fear that came with the knowledge was largely destroyed as it came. There was no sudden overwhelming sense of danger that passed through thought so quickly that it was difficult to catch up and grapple with it – no need for the warning to 'be not afraid of sudden fear', such as might have been present had we collided head-on with a crash and a shock that flung everyone out of his bunk to the floor. Everyone had time to give each condition of danger attention as it came along, and the result of their judgement was as if they had said: 'Well, here is this thing to be faced, and we must see it through as quietly as we can.' Quietness and self-control were undoubtedly the two qualities most expressed. There were times when danger loomed more nearly and there was temporarily some excitement – for example when the first rocket went up – but after the first realisation of what it meant, the crowd took hold of the situation and soon gained the same quiet control that was evident at first. As the sense of fear ebbed and flowed, it was so obviously a thing within one's own power to control, that, quite unconsciously realising the absolute necessity of keeping cool, every one for his own safety put away the thought of danger as far as was possible. Then, too, the curious sense of the whole thing being a dream was very prominent: that all were looking on at the scene from a nearby vantage point in a position of perfect safety, and that those who walked the decks or tied one another's lifebelts on were the actors in a scene of which we were but spectators: that the dream would end soon and we should wake up to find the scene had vanished. Many people have had a similar experience in times of danger, but it was very noticeable standing on the *Titanic*'s deck. I remember observing it particularly while tying on a lifebelt for a man on the deck. It is fortunate that it should be so: to be able to survey such a scene dispassionately is a wonderful aid in the destruction of the fears that go with it. One thing that helped considerably to establish this orderly condition of affairs was the quietness of the surroundings. It may seem weariness to refer again to this, but I am convinced it had much to do with keeping everyone calm. The ship was motionless; there was not a breath of wind; the sky was clear; the sea like a millpond – the general 'atmosphere' was peaceful, and all on board responded unconsciously to it. But what controlled the situation principally was the quality of obedience and respect for authority which is a dominant characteristic of the Teutonic race. Passengers did as they were told by the officers in charge: women went to the decks below, men remained where they were told and waited in silence for the next order, knowing instinctively that this was the only way to bring about the best result for all on board. The officers, in their turn, carried out the work assigned to them by their superior officers as quickly and orderly as circumstances permitted, the senior ones being in control of the manning, filling and lowering of the lifeboats, while the junior officers were lowered in individual boats to take command of the fleet adrift on the sea. Similarly, the engineers below, the band, the gymnasium instructor, were all performing their tasks as they came along: orderly, quietly, without question or stopping to consider what was their chance of safety. This correlation on the part of passengers, officers and crew was simply obedience to duty, and it was innate rather than the product of reasoned judgement.

I hope it will not seem to detract in any way from the heroism of those who faced the last plunge of the *Titanic* so courageously when all the boats had gone – if it does, it is the difficulty of expressing an idea in adequate words – to say that their quiet heroism was largely unconscious, temperamental, not a definite choice between two ways of acting. All that was visible on deck before the boats left tended to this conclusion and the testimony of those who went down with the ship and were afterwards rescued is of the same kind.

Certainly it seems to express much more general nobility of character in a race of people – consisting of different nationalities – to find heroism an unconscious quality of the race than to have it arising as an effort of will, to have to bring it out consciously.

It is unfortunate that some sections of the press should seek to chronicle mainly the individual acts of heroism: the collective behaviour of a crowd is of so much more importance to the world and so much more a test – if a test be wanted – of how a race of people behaves. The attempt to record the acts of individuals leads apparently to such false reports as that of Major Butt holding at bay with a revolver a crowd of passengers and shooting them down as they tried to rush the boats, or of Captain Smith shouting, 'Be British,' through a megaphone, and subsequently committing suicide along with First Officer Murdock. It is only a morbid sense of things that would describe such incidents as heroic. Everyone knows that Major Butt was a brave man, but his record of heroism would not be enhanced if he, a trained army officer, were compelled under orders from the captain to shoot down unarmed passengers. It might in other conditions have been necessary, but it would not be heroic. Similarly there could be nothing heroic in Captain Smith or Murdock putting an end to their lives. It is conceivable men might be so overwhelmed by the sense of disaster that they knew not how they were acting; but to be really heroic would have been to stop with the ship – as of course they did – with the hope of being picked up along with passengers and crew and returning to face an enquiry and to give evidence that would be of supreme value to the whole world for the prevention of similar disasters. It was not possible; but if heroism consists in doing the greatest good to the greatest number, it would have been heroic for both officers to *expect* to be saved. We do not know what they thought, but I, for one, like to imagine that they did so. Second Officer Lightoller worked steadily at the boats until the last possible moment, went down with the ship, was saved in what seemed a miraculous manner, and returned to give valuable evidence before the commissions of two countries.

The second thing that stands out prominently in the emotions produced by the disaster is that in moments of urgent need men and women turn for help to something entirely outside themselves. I remember reading some years ago a story of an atheist who was the guest at dinner of a regimental mess in India. The colonel listened to his remarks on atheism in silence, and invited him for a drive the following morning. He took his guest up a rough mountain road in a light carriage drawn by two ponies, and when some distance from the plain below, turned the carriage round and allowed the ponies to run away – as it seemed – downhill. In the terror of approaching disaster, the atheist was lifted out of his reasoned convictions and prayed aloud for help, when the colonel reined in his ponies, and with the remark that the whole drive had been planned with the intention of proving to his guest that there was a power outside his own reason, descended quietly to level ground.

The story may or may not be true, and in any case is not introduced as an attack on atheism, but it illustrates in a striking way the frailty of dependence on a man's own power and resource in imminent danger. To those men standing on the top deck with the boats all lowered, and still more so when the boats had all left, there came the realisation that human resources were exhausted and human avenues of escape closed. With it came the appeal to whatever consciousness each had of a Power that had created the universe. After all, some Power had made the brilliant stars above, countless millions of miles away, moving in definite order, formed on a definite plan and obeying a definite law: had made each one of the passengers with ability to think and act; with the best proof, after all, of being created – the knowledge of their own existence; and now, if at any time, was the time to appeal to that Power. When the boats had left and it was seen the ship was going down rapidly, men stood in groups on the deck engaged in prayer, and later, as some of them lay on the overturned collapsible boat, they repeated together over and over again the Lord's Prayer – irrespective of religious beliefs, some, perhaps, without religious beliefs, united in a common appeal for deliverance from their surroundings. And this was not because it was a habit, because they had learned this prayer 'at their mother's knee': men do not do such things through habit. It must have been because each one saw removed the thousand and one ways in which he had relied on human, material things to help him – including even dependence on the overturned boat with its bubble of air inside, which any moment a rising swell might remove as it tilted the boat too far sideways, and sink the boat below the surface – saw laid bare his utter dependence on something that had made him and given him power to think – whether he named it God or Divine Power or First Cause or Creator, or named it not at all but recognised it unconsciously – saw these things and expressed them in the form of words he was best acquainted with in common with his fellow men. He did so, not through a sense of duty to his particular religion, not because he had learned the words, but because he recognised that it was the most practical thing to do – the thing best fitted to help him. Men do practical things in times like that: they would not waste a moment on mere words if those words were not an expression of the most intensely real conviction of which they were capable. Again, like the feeling of heroism, this appeal is innate and intuitive, and it certainly has its foundation on a knowledge – largely concealed, no doubt – of immortality. I think this must be obvious: there could be no other explanation of such a general sinking of all the emotions of the human mind expressed in a thousand different ways by a thousand different people in favour of this single appeal.

The behaviour of people during the hours in the lifeboats, the landing on the *Carpathia*, the life there and the landing in New York, can all be summarised by saying that people did not act at all as they were expected to act – or rather as most people expected they would act, and in some cases have erroneously said they did act. Events were there to be faced, and not to crush people down. Situations arose which demanded courage, resource, and in the cases of those who had lost friends most dear to them, enormous self-control; but very wonderfully they responded. There was the same quiet demeanour and poise, the same inborn dominion over circumstances, the same conformity to a normal standard which characterised the crowd of passengers on the deck of the *Titanic* – and for the same reasons.

The first two or three days ashore were undoubtedly rather trying to some of the survivors. It seemed as if coming into the world again – the four days shut off from any news seemed a long time – and finding what a shock the disaster had produced, the flags half-mast, the staring headlines, the sense of gloom noticeable everywhere, made things worse than they had been on the *Carpathia*. The difference in 'atmosphere' was very marked, and people gave way to some extent under it and felt the reaction. Gratitude for their deliverance and a desire to 'make the best of things' must have helped soon, however, to restore them to normal conditions. It is not at all surprising that some survivors felt quieter on the *Carpathia* with its lack of news from the outside world, if the following extract from a leading New York evening paper was some of the material of which the 'atmosphere' on shore was composed:

Stunned by the terrific impact, the dazed passengers rushed from their staterooms into the main saloon amid the crash of splintering steel, rending of plates and shattering of girders, while the boom of falling pinnacles of ice upon the broken deck of the great vessel added to the horror ... In a wild ungovernable mob they poured out of the saloons to witness one of the most appalling scenes possible to conceive ... For a hundred feet the bow was a shapeless mass of bent, broken and splintered steel and iron.

And so on, horror piled on horror, and not a word of it true, or remotely approaching the truth.

This paper was selling in the streets of New York while the *Carpathia* was coming into dock, while relatives of those on board were at the docks to meet them and anxiously buying any paper that might contain news. No one on the *Carpathia* could have supplied such information; there was no one else in the world at that moment who knew any details of the *Titanic* disaster, and the only possible conclusion is that the whole thing was a deliberate fabrication to sell the paper.

This is a repetition of the same defect in human nature noticed in the provision of safety appliances on board ship – the lack of consideration for the other man. The remedy is the same – the law: it should be a criminal offence for anyone to disseminate deliberate falsehoods that cause fear and grief. The moral responsibility of the press is very great, and its duty of supplying the public with only clean, correct news is correspondingly heavy. If the general public is not yet prepared to go so far as to stop the publication of such news by refusing to buy those papers that publish it, then the law should be enlarged to include such cases. Libel is an offence, and this is very much worse than any libel could ever be.

It is only right to add that the majority of the New York papers were careful only to report such news as had been obtained legitimately from survivors or from *Carpathia* passengers. It was sometimes exaggerated and sometimes not true at all, but from the point of reporting what was heard, most of it was quite correct.

One more thing must be referred to – the prevalence of superstitious beliefs concerning the *Titanic*. I suppose no ship ever left port with so much miserable nonsense showered on her. In the first place, there is no doubt many people refused to sail on her because it was her maiden voyage, and this apparently is a common superstition: even the clerk of the White Star Office where I purchased my ticket admitted it was a reason that prevented people from sailing. A number of people have written to the press to say they had thought of sailing on her, or had decided to sail on her, but because of 'omens' cancelled the passage. Many referred to the sister ship, the *Olympic*, pointed to the 'ill luck' that they say has dogged her – her collision with the *Hawke*, and a second mishap necessitating repairs and a wait in harbour, where passengers deserted her; they prophesied even greater disaster for the *Titanic*, saying they would not dream of travelling on the boat. Even some aboard were very nervous, in an undefined way. One lady said she had never wished to take this boat, but her friends had insisted and bought her ticket and she had not had a happy moment since. A friend told me of the voyage of the *Olympic* from Southampton after the wait in harbour, and said there was a sense of gloom pervading the whole ship: the stewards and stewardesses even going so far as to say it was a *'death-ship'*. This crew, by the way, was largely transferred to the *Titanic*.

The incident with the *New York* at Southampton, the appearance of the stoker at Queenstown in the funnel, combine with all this to make a mass of nonsense in which apparently sensible people believe, or which at any rate they discuss. Correspondence is published with an official of the White Star Line from someone imploring them not to name the new ship 'Gigantic', because it seems like 'tempting fate' when the *Titanic* has been sunk. It would seem almost as if we were back in the Middle Ages when witches were burned because they kept black cats. There seems no more reason why a black stoker should be an ill omen for the *Titanic* than a black cat should be for an old woman.

The only reason for referring to these foolish details is that a surprisingly large number of people think there may be 'something in it'. The effect is this: that if a ship's company and a number of passengers get imbued with that undefined dread of the unknown – the relics no doubt of the savage's fear of what he does not understand – it has an unpleasant effect on the harmonious working of the ship: the officers and crew feel the depressing influence, and it may even spread so far as to prevent them being as alert and keen as they otherwise would; may even result in some duty not being as well done as usual. Just as the unconscious demand for speed and haste to get across the Atlantic may have tempted captains to take a risk they might otherwise not have done, so these gloomy forebodings may have more effect sometimes than we imagine. Only a little thing is required sometimes to weigh down the balance for and against a certain course of action.

At the end of this chapter of mental impressions it must be recorded that one impression remains constant with us all today – that of the deepest gratitude that we came safely through the wreck of the *Titanic*; and its corollary – that our legacy from the wreck, our debt to those who were lost with her, is to see, as far as in us lies, that such things are impossible ever again. Meanwhile we can say of them, as Shelley, himself the victim of a similar disaster, says of his friend Keats in 'Adonais':

Peace, peace! he is not dead, he doth not sleep,
He hath awakened from the dream of life …
He lives, he wakes –' T is Death is dead, not he;
Mourn not for Adonais.

List of Illustrations

1. © Amberley Archive.
2. © Amberley Archive.
3. © Amberley Archive.
4. © Amberley Archive.
5. © Jonathan Reeve JR2275b101p313T 1912.
6. © Jonathan Reeve JR2279b101p316L 1912.
7. © Jonathan Reeve JR2277b101p314T 1912.
8. © Jonathan Reeve JR2276b101p313B 1912.
9. © Jonathan Reeve JR2311f185 1912.
10. © Jonathan Reeve JR2315f141det1 1912.
11. © Jonathan Reeve JR2132f122 1912.
12. © Jonathan Reeve JR2139f129 1912.
13. © Jonathan Reeve JR2315f189 1912.
14. © Jonathan Reeve JR2315f141det2 1912.
15. © Jonathan Reeve JR2188b98fp137 1912.
16. © Amberley Archive.
17. © Jonathan Reeve JR2280b101p316R 1912.
18. © Jonathan Reeve JR2363f212 1912.
19. © Amberley Archive.
20. © Jonathan Reeve JR2221f147 1912.
21. © Jonathan Reeve JR2119f109 1912.
22. © Jonathan Reeve JR2253f161 1912.
23. © Jonathan Reeve JR2313f187 1912.
24. © Jonathan Reeve JR2140f130 1912.
25. © Jonathan Reeve JR2355f204 1912.
26. © Jonathan Reeve JR2329f203 1912.
27. © Jonathan Reeve JR2268f176 1912.
28. © Jonathan Reeve JR2356f205 1912.
29. © Jonathan Reeve JR2272f180 1912.
30. & 31. © Jonathan Reeve JR1996f24 1912 and © Jonathan Reeve JR1990f18 1912.
32. © Jonathan Reeve JR2317f191 1912.
33. © Jonathan Reeve JR1993f21 1912.
34. © Jonathan Reeve JR2358f207 1912.
35, 36, 37, 38, 39 & 40. © Jonathan Reeve JR2195b98p201TL 1912, © Jonathan Reeve JR2196b98p201ML 1912, © Jonathan Reeve JR2197b98p201BL 1912, © Jonathan Reeve JR2198b98p201TR 1912, © Jonathan Reeve JR2199b98p201MR 1912, © Jonathan Reeve JR2200b98p201BR 1912.
41. © Jonathan Reeve JR2014f42 1912.
42. © Jonathan Reeve JR2078f68 1912.
43. © Jonathan Reeve JR2016f44 1912.
44. © Jonathan Reeve JR2017f45 1912.
45. © Jonathan Reeve JR2251b100p251 1912.
46, 47, 48 & 49. © Jonathan Reeve JR2206b98fp233 1912, © Jonathan Reeve JR2122f112 1912, © Jonathan Reeve JR2091f81 1912 and © Jonathan Reeve JR2174b98fp40 1912.
50, 51 & 52. © Jonathan Reeve JR2323f197 1912, © Jonathan Reeve JR2109f99 1912 and © Jonathan Reeve JR2108f98 1912.
53. © Jonathan Reeve JR2094f84 1912.
54. © Jonathan Reeve JR2360f209 1912.
55. © Jonathan Reeve JR2023f53 1912.
56. © Jonathan Reeve JR2089f79 1912.
57. © Jonathan Reeve JR2027f57 1912.
58. © Jonathan Reeve JR2024f54 1912.
59. © Jonathan Reeve JR2250f160 1912.
60. © Jonathan Reeve JR2141f131 1912.
61. © Jonathan Reeve JR2361f210 1912.
62. © Jonathan Reeve JR2366f215 1912.
63. © Jonathan Reeve JR2359f208 1912.
64. © Jonathan Reeve JR2072f62 1912.
65. © Jonathan Reeve JR2103f93 1912.
66. © Nicholas Wade.
67. © Nicholas Wade.
68. © Jonathan Reeve JR2367b107p68 1912.

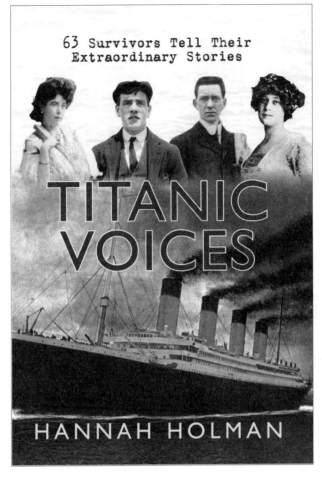

Titanic History from Amberley Publishing

TITANIC
W.B. Bartlett

'Enthralling' THE DAILY MAIL

'Quite the best and most level-headed telling of the whole story I have ever read' THE INDEPENDENT ON SUNDAY

£20.00	978-1-84868-422-5	368 pages HB 72 illus, 14 col
£9.99	978-1-4456-0482-4	368 pages PB 72 illus, 14 col

A GIRL ABOARD THE TITANIC
Eva Hart

The remarkable memoir of Eva Hart, a 7-year old passenger on the doomed Titanic.

£16.99   978-1-4456-0089-5   256 pages HB 60 illus

I SURVIVED THE TITANIC
Lawrence Beesley

'The best first-hand account of a passenger's experiences... a first-rate piece of descriptive writing' THE GUARDIAN

'The clearest account given by any survivor of the disaster' THE DAILY MAIL

£16.99   978-1-4456-0043-5   192 pages HB 67 illus

TITANIC VOICES
63 Survivors Tell Their Extraordinary Stories
Hannah Holman

The sinking of the Titanic in the words of the survivors.

£20.00   978-1-4456-0222-6   512 pages HB 135 illus, 11 col

TITANIC
Filson Young

'If you only read one book about Titanic, read this one; if you've read every book published about the Titanic, read this one again' NAUTILUS INTERNATIONAL TELEGRAPH

£16.99   978-1-4456-0407-7
160 pages HB 60 illus

THE TRUTH ABOUT THE TITANIC
Archibald Gracie

'Very vivid... the truth about the Titanic' NEW YORK TIMES

The classic account by passenger Archibald Gracie who survived on top of an upturned lifeboat. With a new introduction and rare images.

£8.99   978-1-4456-0594-4
240 pages PB 76 illus

THE ILLUSTRATED SINKING OF THE TITANIC
L.T. Myers

America's first 'instant book' about the sinking of the Titanic.

£17.99   978-1-84868-053-1
192 pages PB 78 illus

WHY THE TITANIC SANK
W. B. Bartlett

Although the answer appears obvious, there is far more to the sinking of the Titanic than is popularly understood.

Feb 2012 £12.99   978-1-4456-0630-9
192 pages PB 50 illus

TITANIC
Campbell McCutcheon

The ideal introduction to the history and fate of the Titanic.

Feb 2012 £4.99   978-1-4456-0415-2
32 pages PB 78 illus, 30 col

TITANIC HERO
Arthur Rostron

'A gem... Arthur Rostron was actually there, and his account is about real people and the practicalities of helping them' NAUTILUS INTERNATIONAL TELEGRAPH

£17.99   978-1-4456-0420-6
192 pages PB 39 illus

Available from all good bookshops or to order direct
Please call 01453-847-800 www.amberleybooks.com